George C. Gilmore

State Senators 1784-1900

New Hampshire Men at Bunker Hill, June 17, 1775

George C. Gilmore

State Senators 1784-1900
New Hampshire Men at Bunker Hill, June 17, 1775

ISBN/EAN: 9783337154110

Printed in Europe, USA, Canada, Australia, Japan

Cover: Foto ©ninafisch / pixelio.de

More available books at **www.hansebooks.com**

STATE SENATORS

1784-1900

NEW HAMPSHIRE MEN AT BUNKER HILL

JUNE 17, 1775

BY GEORGE C. GILMORE

MANCHESTER, N. H.
PRINTED BY THE JOHN B. CLARKE COMPANY
1899

INTRODUCTION.

This number of the manual is compiled for the use of the last legislature to be convened in the present century. The early pages present the names, alphabetically arranged, of all the members of the state senate from the adoption of a permanent constitution in 1784 to the present time, including the senate elected in 1898. During this period there have been ninety-five annual sessions of twelve senators, and eleven biennial sessions of twenty-four senators. There have been 1,412 elections to the senate, and noting re-elections and contested elections it appears that 762 different persons have held seats in the senate of this state. The early pages of this volume were printed before the organization of the present senate. The name of the president will appear in the later pages.

The following table and the lists of New Hampshire men at Bunker Hill were prepared by Hon. George C. Gilmore of Manchester, N. H.

STATE SENATORS FROM 1784 TO 1900.

Asterisk indicates President of the Senate.

Name.	Residence.	Service.	Died.	Year.	Age.	Mo.	Days.
Abbot, Daniel	Nashua	1831	Dec. 3	1853	70	9	9
Abbott, Henry	Winchester	1873–1854	Feb. 12	1888	65		
Abbott, Timothy	Wilton	1846	Oct. 27	1866	86	1	26
Adams, Cyrus	Grafton	1861–1862	Dec. 4	1865	70	4	27
Adams, Daniel N.	Mont Vernon	1838–9–40	June 8	1864	90	9	
Adams, George H.	Springfield	1850–1851	July 21	1886	84		
Adams, William	Plymouth	1899–1900					
Albee, Ellery	Londonderry	1869–10–14–12–13					
Alcock, Robert	Winchester	1869–1876	Oct.	1828	75		
Aldrich, George	Deering	1804–5–6–7	May 17	1830	87		
Allen, Amasa	Westmoreland	1805–6–7–8	July 1	1815	77		
Allen, John J., jr.	Walpole	1904	July	1821	69		
Amidon, Charles J.	Fitzwilliam	1861–1862	June 20	1884	66		
Amsden, Charles H.	Hinsdale	1878–9–80					
Ashley, Horace S.	Concord	1883–1884					
Atherton, Joshua	Nashua	1897–1898	April 3	1809	71	9	13
Atkinson, George	Amherst	1792–1793	Jan. 13	1865	66		
Atkinson, Daniel C	Portsmouth	1785–6–7	April 5	1842	56	7	8
Badger, William *	Sanbornton	1819	Sept. 21	1852	73		9
Bailey, Joshua	Gilmanton	1814–15–16	April 9	1806	68	11	12
Bailey, John H.	Hopkinton	1787	Oct. 23	1879	55		
Bailey, Henry A.	Portsmouth	1869					
Baker, Moses	Manchester	1887–1888					
Baker, Otis	Campton	1794–5–6–7–8–9	April 6	1862	65		
Baker, Henry M.	Dover	1785–1786	Oct. 27	1891	73		
Baker, William D.	Bow	1891–1892					
	Runney	1895–1896					

STATE SENATORS FROM 1784 TO 1900.

Name	Place	Years	Month	Year		
Balcom, George L.	Claremont	1889–1890				
Barker, Thaddeus W.	Nelson	1895–1896				
Barker, Tileston A.	Westmoreland	1871–1872				
Barnard, Benjamin	South Hampton	1806–1807	Dec.	1879	9	14
Barnard, Daniel*	Franklin	1865–1866	March	1852	11	18
Barney, John W.	Lancaster	1868–1869	Jan.	1892	1	16
Barrett, Charles	New Ipswich	1791–3–4	March	1883		
Barrett, James J.	Littleton	1872	Sept.	1808		17
Barton, Cyrus	Concord	1833–1834	Aug.	1885	6	17
Barton, Levi W.	Newport	1857–1868	Feb.	1855	1	23
Bartlett, Josiah*	Kingston	1809–10–24				
Bartlett, James	Dover	1827–1828	April	1838		4
Bartlett, Bradbury	Nottingham	1821–1822	July	1837	11	
Bartlett, Charles H.*	Manchester	1882–1883	Sept.	1869	7	10
Bartlett, John P.	Manchester	1885–1886				
Batcheller, James	Marlborough	1842–50–51	April	1866	4	14
Batchelder, Daniel	Wilton	1839–1830	May	1853	1	19
Beal, Joseph R.	Keene	1891–1892	Jan.	1895	8	1
Bean, Benning M.*	Moultonborough	1824–5–6–31–32	Feb.	1866	3	2
Belding, Elijah	Swanzey	1820–40–41	Nov.	1867	3	16
Bell, John	Londonderry	1788–7–8–9–90	Nov.	1825	10	4
Bell, John, Jr.	Londonderry	1803	March	1836	11	15
Bell, Samuel*	Francestown	1807–1808	Dec.	1850		24
Bell, Charles H.*	Exeter	1863–1864	Nov.	1893		
Bellows, John	Walpole	1785–6–7–92–3–4	Aug.	1812		
Bellows, Josiah	Walpole	1813	June	1846	4	
Bennett, Asahel H.	Winchester	1852–1853	July	1880	7	29
Bennett, John S.	Newmarket	1859	Nov.	1875		27
Berry, Nathaniel S.	Bristol	1833–1836	April	1894		
Berry, Jonathan F.	Barrington	1885–1886	Jan.	1822	4	27
Betton, Silas	Salem	1800–1–2	March	1859	11	20
Bingham, James H.	Alstead	1816–17–22	Jan.	1885	8	28
Bingham, George A.	Littleton	1864–1865				
Bingham, Harry	Littleton	1883–4–5–6	Oct.	1862	11	25
Bixby, William	Francestown	1829–1830	June	1849		26
Blair, Walter	Plymouth	1835–1836	May	1872	10	
Blair, William N.	Laconia	1870				

8   NEW HAMPSHIRE MANUAL.

Name.	Residence.	Service.	Died.	Year.	Age.	Mos.	Days.
Blair, Henry W	Plymouth	1867–1868	Jan. 10	1833	71		
Blaisdell, Daniel	Canaan	1814–1815	Aug. 24	1875	69		
Blaisdell, Daniel	Hanover	1863–1864	Feb. 14	1864	66		17
Blake, Joseph	Raymond	1859–1860	March 7	1833	80		
Blanchard, Joseph	Chester	1794–5–6–7–8–9	Oct. 5	1872			
Blodgett, Caleb	Dorchester	1833–1834					
Blodgett, Isaac N	Franklin	1879–1880					
Blood, Francis	Temple	1784					
Blunt, Edward O	Nashua	1887–1888	April 14	1814	79	8	11
Boardman, Langley	Portsmouth	1822–3–31	July 31	1896	49		
Bodwell, Loring B	Manchester	1897–1898		1833	59		
Bowers, Jesse	Nashua	1825–6–7	June 24	1854	74		
Bowers, Sheperd L	Newport	1893–1894	Oct. 14	1894	66	11	2
Boyden, Frederick	Hinsdale	1855	Nov. 11	1871	61		
Bradley, John	Concord	1894–5–6–7–8	July 6	1815	72		
Bradley, Moses H	Bristol	1854	June 22	1834	52	3	8
Brackett, Asa M	Wakefield	1885–1886					
Briggs, James F	Manchester	1876 1 2					
Britton, Abiathar G	Orford	1842	Dec. 14	1855	77		
Brodhead, John	Newmarket	1815–18–19–20–7–8	April 17	1838	65	11	20
Brooks, Charles F	Westmoreland	1857–1858	Nov. 4	1879	74		
Broughton, John H	Portsmouth	1879–1880					
Brown, Abel	South Hampton	1833–1834	Nov. 13	1878	83	9	3
Brown, Abram	Hopkinton	1899–1900	Dec. 15	1852			
Brown, Frank P	Whitefield	1899–1900					
Brown, Titus*	Francestown	1842–1843	Jan. 29	1849	62	11	20
Brown, Warren	Hampton Falls	1872–1873					
Brown, Manson S	Plymouth	1885–1886					
Brown, Edmund H	Concord	1895–1896					
Buford, Marcellus	Portsmouth	1855	April 19	1894	76	5	6
Buffum, Joseph	Westmoreland	1818	Nov. 29	1829	74	1	
Buffum, David H*	Somersworth	1877–1878	Dec. 7	1882	62	1	20
Burleigh, Micajah C	Somersworth	1857–1858	March	1881	63		23

STATE SENATORS FROM 1784 TO 1900.

Name	Town	Term					
Burleigh, George W.	Somersworth			1865–1866			
Burgin, Hall	Allenstown			1825–6–8	1844		15
Burnham, John	Hopkinton	April	12	1861–1862	1867	5	13
Burnham, Henry L.	Dunbarton	April	30	1864–1865	1893	5	6
Burnap, James	Marlow	April	28	1876–1877	1894		
Burns, Robert	Hebron	June	26	1851–1852	1866		
Burns, William	Lancaster	April	2	1856–1857	1885	11	8
Burns, William A.	Rumney	June	21	1860–1861	1886		
Burns, Charles H.	Wilton			1873–9–80			
Buswell, Oliver B.	Grantham	July	27	1854	1892	11	28
Butler, Henry	Nottingham	July	20	1800	1813		
Butler, George S.	Pelham			1884–1886			
Buxton, Willis G.	Boscawen			1897–1898			
Buzzell, Hezekiah D.	Weare			1822			
Campbell, Charles H.*	Nashua	Aug.	22	1871–1872	1858	3	29
Campbell, Zebulon F.	Landaff			1857–1858	1895		
Carleton, Peter	Swanzey	April	29	1906	1828	10	2
Carpenter, Elijah	Gofstown	Oct.	24	1852–1873	1861	1	14
Carr, Jesse	Gofstown	Nov.	19	1875–1876	1874	1	20
Carr, Alonzo F.	Andover	Dec.	16	1857–1888	1887	11	26
Carr, Robert C.	Haverhill	Feb.	22	1855–30–1	1892	11	10
Cartland, Samuel*	Lebanon	Feb.	24		1852		
Carter, William S.	Northfield			1891–1892			
Cate, Asa P.*	Northwood	Dec.	12	1844–1845	1874	6	12
Cate, Charles F.	Middleton			1879–1880			
Chadwick, John	Fitzwilliam	Sept.	16	1829	1853	8	10
Chamberlain, Levi	Keene	Aug.	31	1820–1830	1868	3	18
Chamberlain, William P.	Bedford			1885–1886			
Chandler, Thomas	Manchester	Jan.	28	1817–18–25–6–7	1866	5	18
Chandler, George B.	Cornish			1874			
Chase, Moses	Conway	Oct.	18	1785–1788	1799	10	9
Chase, Jonathan T.	Milford	Sept.	5	1835–1836	1870	10	1
Chase, Leonard	Kingston	June	7	1861–1862	1868		
Chase, Amos C.	Manchester			1881–1882			
Chatel, Joseph P.	Plainfield	Nov.	27	1899–1900	1888	11	1
Chellis, John P.	Lebanon			1857–1858			
Cheney, Elias H.				1885–1886			

10 NEW HAMPSHIRE MANUAL.

Name.	Residence.	Service.	Died.	Year.	Age.	Mos.	Days.
Cheney, Thomas P	Ashland	1889–1890					
Cheney, Harry M	Lebanon	1897–1898					
Cilley, Joseph	Nottingham	1790–1795	Aug. 25	1799	65	4	15
Clark, James	Franklin	1835–1836	June 15	1861	77	8	15
Clark, William	Campton	1849–1850	April 5	1878	66	8	16
Clark, Peter H	New Ipswich	1885–1886	Aug. 26	1891	74	3	11
Clarke, Greenleaf	Atkinson	1879–1880	Aug. 18	1888	72		
Clarke, Nathaniel H	Plaistow	1885–1886					
Clarke, Frank G	Peterborough	1889–1890					
Claggett, William	Portsmouth	1825	Dec. 28	1870	80		21
Cleaves, Samuel	Portsmouth	1838	April 5	1873	81		
Clough, Joseph 2d	Loudon	1849–1850	Nov. 1	1860	56		
Clough, John	Enfield	1857–1858	Oct. 5	1869	68		
Clough, Joseph M	New London	1881–1882					
Cloutman, John F	Farmington	1876–1877					
Cobleigh, Wayne	Northumberland	1875–1876	May 7	1878	85	6	14
Cochran, Robert B	New Boston	1854–1856	Jan. 28	1826	74		
Cogswell, Amos	Dover	1857–58–59	Aug.	1855			
Cogswell, Pearson	Gilmanton	1823	June 18	1848	66		
Cogswell, Amos	Canterbury	1858–1859					
Cogswell, Thomas	Gilmanton	1878	Sept. 16	1825	38		
Colby, Thomas W	Hopkinton	1823	Oct. 9	1844	47	1	19
Colby, Simon P	Weare	1842–1843					
Colby, Ira, Jr	Claremont	1869–1870					
Collins, Alfred A	Danville	1899–1900					
Collins, John S	Gilsum	1885–1886					
Collins, Charles N	Nashua	1891–1892					
Colman, Dudley C	Brookfield	1879–1880	March 20	1843	65	8	7
Cooledge, Henry	Keene	1837	June 7	1894	65	7	23
Cooledge, Cornelius	Hillsborough	1879–80–1–2	April 16	1880	86	4	10
Comerford, John	Sanbornton	1839–1840	Aug. 8	1852	52		
Cook, Benaiah	Keene	1844	April 14	1890	86	8	27
Cooper, Lemuel P	Croydon	1861–1862					

STATE SENATORS FROM 1784 TO 1900.

Name	Town	Years					
Conn, William	Portsmouth	1889–1890		Nov.	6	1889	71	2	22
*Corbin, Austin	Newport	1853–1854		June	14	1876	84	6	17
Corning, Charles R.	Concord	1889–1890							
Cox, Alfred A.	Enfield	1881–1882							
Cram, Charles T.	Pittsfield	1871							
Creighton, James B.*	Newmarket	1889–1890		Aug.	11	1882	92	10	24
Cross, Ephraim	Lancaster	1844–1845		Sept.	7	1876	81	6	20
Cummings, William H	Lisbon	1877–1878		July	15	1891	74	6	6
Cummings, George W.	Francestown	1881–2–3–4							
Cummings, George A.	Concord	1891–1892							
Currier, Moody*	Manchester	1854		Aug.	23	1898	92	4	2
Currier, Frank D.*	Canaan	1887–1888							
Curtice, Grovenor A.	Hopkinton	1881–1882							
Dame, Richard	Rochester	1837–1838		Sept.	19	1828	72		
Dame, John	Lyme	1829		Feb.	28	1830			
Dame, Jeremiah	Farmington	1848–1849		Sept.	8	1855			
Damon, Charles H	Campton	1883–1884							
Danforth, Charles C	Concord	1889–1890							
Daniell, Warren F.	Franklin	1875–1876							
Darling, Joshua*	Henniker	1808–9–10–11–12–13–14–15		May	16	1842	65		4
Davis, Reuben	Cornish	1844–1845		March	7	1869	76		
Davis, George G.	Marlborough	1883–1884							
Davis, Walter S.	Hopkinton	1885–1886							
Davis, Murray	Chesterfield	1885–1886		March	20	1888	42	3	4
Dearborn, Joseph J	Deerfield	1865–1866		Feb.	19	1890	77	11	11
Denneritt, Stephen	Durham	1845		June	27	1867	60	6	9
Dinsmore, Thomas	Alstead	1883–1884							
Dodge, George H.	Hampton Falls	1846		Feb.	14	1862	54		14
Dow, Moses*	Haverhill	1784–1791		March	31	1811	65	8	
Dow, Samuel P.	Newmarket	1858		Dec.	7	1875	60	2	7
Dow, Israel	Manchester	1883–1884		Aug.	24	1898	82	7	
Dow, Perry H.	Manchester	1891–1892							
Drake, James	Pittsfield	1847–1848		April	5	1870	64		9
Drew, Thomas C.	Walpole	1811–20–21		April	12	1843	81		
Drew, Irving W.	Lancaster	1883–1884		March	22	1888	79	11	17
Drew, Amos W.	Stewartstown	1862–1863		March	24	1863	78	9	10
Drowne, Daniel P.	Portsmouth	1832–1833							

12   NEW HAMPSHIRE MANUAL.

Name.	Residence.	Service.	Died.	Year.	Age.	Mos.	Days.
Dudley, Jason H.	Colebrook	1891-1892					
Durgin, Frank H.	Newmarket	1897-1898					
Duncan, John	Antrim	1797	Feb. 14	1823	88		10
Durkee, John	Hanover	1816-18-19	Sept. 9	1846	85	11	
Dyer, Samuel B.	London	1837	Nov. 19	1846	67	7	28
Eastman, Nehemiah	Farmington	1820-4-2-3-4	Jan. 19	1856	70	7	
Eastman, Josiah C.	Hampstead	1853-1854	Nov. 27	1897	86		6
Eastman, George S.	Manchester	1887-1888					
Eastman, Edwin G.	Exeter	1889-1890					
Eaton, Leonard	Warner	1853-1854	Nov. 22	1868	68	3	13
Eaton, Hosea	New Ipswich	1859-1860	Nov. 26	1879	59	3	
Eaton, Harrison	Amherst	1855	March 9	1889	71		
Edgerly, James A.	Somersworth	1895-1896					
Edgerton, Samuel	Langdon	1833-1834	March 27	1854	65	3	19
Eldridge, Marcellus	Portsmouth	1893-1894	March 12	1898	59		
Ellis, Bertram	Keene	1899-1900					
Ellis, Caleb	Claremont	1811	May 9	1816	49	9	20
Emerson, Daniel	Hollis	1795	Oct. 4	1820	73	1	5
Emerson, Bodwell	Hopkinton	1828-1829	Dec. 29	1838	65		23
Emerson, Abraham	Candia	1840-1841	Oct. 18	1891	91		
Emerson, Edward P.	Nashua	1843-1844	Feb. 24	1882	73		
Emerson, Samuel	Moultonborough	1859	March 4	1872			
Emery, John W.	Portsmouth	1897-1898					
Emmons, Gardner B.	Concord	1897-1898					
Evans, Benjamin	Warner	1840	Nov. 12	1844	72	4	13
Evans, Pearson G.	Gorham	1883-1894					
Fairbanks, George H.	Newport	1881-1882					
Fairbanks, Alfred G.	Manchester	1893-1894	May 28	1896	74		
Fairfield, John	Lyme	1807-8-9-10	April 1	1827	76		25
Farrar, William H.	Somersworth	1874	Feb. 21	1876	59		9
Farrington, James	Rochester	1832-3-4	Oct. 29	1859	68		
Faulkner, Frederick A.	Keene	1891-1888					
Felker, Samuel D.	Rochester	1891-1892					

STATE SENATORS FROM 1784 TO 1900.

Name	Town	Years	Month	Day	Year			
Fellows, James G.	Pembroke	1897–1898						
Field, John H.	Nashua	1899–1900					1	14
Fisk, William	Amherst	1810–11–12–13	June	4	1831	76		
Fisk, Samuel	Claremont	1815	Dec.	29	1834	65	4	1
Fisk, Levi	Jaffrey	1825–1836	Aug.	17	1857	82	5	6
Fisk, Thomas	Dublin	1859–1860	April	30	1889	86		
Fiske, Amos F.	Marlow	1862–1864	Jan.	6	1873	65		
Flanders, James	Warner	1784–5–6–7–8, 1800–1–2–3	Jan.	8	1820	80		
Fling, Lewis W.	Bristol	1871–1872						
Floyd, Charles M.	Manchester	1899–1900						
Fogg, Jeremiah	Kensington	1796–7–8–9, 1800–1801	May	26	1808	58		
Folsom, Simeon	Exeter	1812–1813	Aug.	24	1816	52	6	5
Folsom, Charles W.	Rochester	1883–1884	March	5	1892	51	3	7
Folsom, Charles E.	Epping	1895–1896	Feb.	15	1886	51		
Foss, James	Strafham	1847–1848	Sept.	26	1852	71	3	17
Foster, Abiel*	Canterbury	1791–2–3–4	Feb.		1806	74	5	29
Foster, Herman*	Manchester	1860–1861	Feb.	17	1875	39		
Foster, George	Belford	1872–1873	March	21	1881			
Fox, Elbridge W.	Milton	1899–1900						
Fradd, Horatio	Manchester	1891–1892					11	
Freeman, Jonathan	Hanover	1789–90–2–3	Aug.	20	1808	63		
Freeman, Asa	Dover	1851–1852	Dec.	8	1867	79	8	6
Freese, Jacob	Deerfield	1829–1830	Aug.	14	1843	65		
French, Reuben L.	Pittsfield	1870	Dec.	14	1896	78		
French, Francis T.	East Kingston	1883–1884					6	25
French, James E.	Moultonborough	1887–1888	Jan.	4	1893	82	6	6
Frink, Darius	Newington	1865–1866	Sept.	26	1872	81		
Gage, William H.	Boscawen	1846–7–8					7	18
Gallinger, Jacob H.*	Concord	1878–9–80					4	8
Gale, Stephen H.	Exeter	1895–1896						
Gault, Jesse	Hooksett	1885–1886	May	8	1888	64	11	12
George, Charles S.	Barnstead	1887–1888	Jan.	22	1896	79		
Gerrish, Henry	Boscawen	1782–1799	May	16	1806	68		
Gerrish, Enoch	Concord	1887–1888						
Gibson, Jesse	Pelham	1844–1845	Feb.	27	1876	88	8	13
Gilman, Joseph*	Exeter	1784–5–6–7	April		1806	68		
Gilman, John T.	Exeter	1791	Aug.	31	1828	74		

NEW HAMPSHIRE MANUAL.

Name.	Residence.	Service.	Died.	Year.	Age.	Mos.	Days.
Gilman, Nathaniel	Exeter	1792–5–1802	Jan. 26	1847	88		
Gilman, Nicholas*	Exeter	1814	May 2	1814	58	9	
Gilman, Virgil C.	Nashua	1881–1882					
Gilman, Edward H.	Exeter	1887–1888					
Gilmore, Gawen	Acworth	1823–1824	Nov. 21	1841	73		7
Gilmore, Joseph A.*	Concord	1858–1859	April 17	1867	55	10	
Gilmore, George C.	Manchester	1881–1882					
Glidden, John M.	Charlestown	1865–1866	Dec. 19	1873	68		6
Goddard, John	Portsmouth	1801–1802	Dec. 18	1829	73		
Godfrey, Ezekiel	Poplin	1863	June 5	1817	66		
Goodhue, Converse	Enfield	1829–1840	Sept. 14	1867	65		
Goodrich, Moses H.	Portsmouth	1865–1886					
Goodnow, Walter L.	Jaffrey	1883–1884					
Gordon, George H.	Canaan	1899–1900					
Gordon, William	Amherst	1794–1795	May 8	1802	39		
Gordon, Nathaniel*	Exeter	1869–1870					
Gordon, Francis A.	Merrimack	1885–1886					
Gould, John	Dunbarton	1820	Feb. 1	1852	83	5	16
Gould, Ezra	Sandwich	1869	Feb. 26	1888	79	6	
Gould, Marcellus	Manchester	1865–1866					
Gove, Charles F.*	Goffstown	1825	Oct. 21	1859	66	5	9
Gove, John, Jr.	Claremont	1827–1839	Jan. 28	1843	50	8	2
Gove, William H.*	Weare	1872–1874	March 11	1876	58		
Gove, Richard	Laconia	1881–1882	April 3	1885	60		
Graves, Rufus E.	Brentwood	1897–1898					
Gray, Augustus W.	Bennington	1889–1890					
Gregg, David A.	Derry	1840–1841	May 15	1866	78		4
Gregg, David A.	Nashua	1889–1890					
Green, Peter	Concord	1787–9–90	March 27	1798	52		
Greenleaf, Abner*	Portsmouth	1829	Sept. 28	1868	82	6	17
Greenleaf, Charles H.	Franconia	1897–1898					
Gustine, Edward	Keene	1879–80–1–2	July 4	1898	78	10	3
Hackett, William H. Y.*	Portsmouth	1861–1862	Aug. 9	1878	77	10	16

STATE SENATORS FROM 1784 TO 1900.

Name	Town	Years	Month	Day	Year			
Hale, William*	Hinsdale	1854–1855	July	22	1876	69		
Hale, Enoch	Rindge	1784	April	9	1813	79	8	13
Hale, Samuel	Barrington	1791–3–4	April	28	1828	89	5	1
Hale, William	Dover	1797–8–9–1800	Nov.	9	1848	84		
Hale, Salma	Keene	1824–1845	Nov.	19	1866	79		
Hale, Isaac	Franklin	1842–1843	June	10	1865	74		
Haley, Abel	Tuftonborough	1850–1851	Aug.	4	1880			
Haley, Levi T	Wolfeborough	1883–1884						
Hall, Elijah	Portsmouth	1807–1808	June	22	1830	87	9	13
Hall, Horace	Charlestown	1829	Oct.	20	1861	82	11	29
Hall, Obed	Tamworth	1834–1836	May	21	1873	78	2	27
Hall, Joshua G	Dover	1871–1872	Oct.	31	1898	69		29
Hall, Jeremiah F	Portsmouth	1874–1875	March	2	1888	71		
Hall, Lafayette	Newmarket	1881–2–3–4	Aug.	26	1885	68		
Hall, Charles E	Greenville	1891–1892						
Ham, William	Portsmouth	1811–12–13–14–15–16	Sept.	3	1845	85		19
Hamilton, Irenus	Lyme	1846	Aug.	19	1876	69		
Hammond, George W	Gilsum	1855–1856	Jan.	30	1872		8	
Hammond, George F	Nashua	1893–1894						
Handerson, Phinehas	Chesterfield	1816–17–25 1831–1832	March	16	1853	74	3	4
Harper, Joseph M*	Canterbury	1829–1830	Jan.	15	1865	78	6	25
Harmon, Artemas	Eaton	1846	Feb.	7	1882	73	4	15
Harris, Milan	Nelson	1863–1864	July	27	1884			
Harriman, Walter	Warner	1859–1860	July	25	1884			
Hartwell, Ephraim	New Ipswich	1795–6–8–9–1800–1801			1816	65		
Hartwell, John	Northwood	1816–1817	May	2	1849	70	5	29
Harvey, Jonathan*	Sutton	1816–17–18–19–20–1–2	Aug.	23	1859	75	9	17
Harvey, Matthew*	Hopkinton	1825–6–7	April	7	1866	79		2
Harvey, George K	Surry	1882–1884	Feb.	19	1898	69		
Hastings, Thomas N	Walpole	1897–8–9–1900						
Hatch, Oscar C	Littleton	1899–1900						
Hatch, Samuel	Exeter	1841–1842	June	7	1843		5	
Hatch, John K	Greenland	1843–1844						
Hatch, Charles W	Greenland	1863–1864	Nov.	8	1870	50	2	14
Hatch, Otis G	Tamworth	1873						
Hatch, John	Greenland	1885–1886						
Hatch, George A	Laconia	1893–1894						

16 NEW HAMPSHIRE MANUAL.

Name.	Residence.	Services.	Died.		Year.	Age.	Mos.	Days.
Hayes, John M.	Salisbury	1867–1868	Jan.	10	1880	56	10	25
Hayes, Luther	Milton	1879–1880	March	28	1885	75		
Haynes, Elbridge G.	Manchester	1879–1880	Nov.	3	1881	66	9	5
Head, Natt*	Hooksett	1876–1877	Nov.	12	1883	55	5	23
Henley, Newell	Kensington	1821	July	27	1880	71		
Healey, Joseph	Washington	1824	Oct.	10	1866	82		
Herring, George M.	Farmington	1855–1856	Sept.	27	1875	63		
Hersey, Charles H.	Keene	1887–1888						
Hewes, Sylvanus	Lyme	1845–1847	Aug.	28	1880	91	3	21
Hibbard, Harry*	Bath	1846–7–8	July	28	1872	56	1	28
Higgins, Freeman	Manchester	1893–1894						
Hill, Isaac	Concord	1820–1–2–27	March	22	1851	63		
Hinds, William H. W.	Milford	1885–1886	July	29	1897	68	11	28
Hitchcock, Henry A.	Walpole	1872–1873	Jan.	4	1870	63		
Hobbs, Moody	Pelham	1855–1856	Aug.	28	1880	71	3	19
Hobbs, Edwin H	Manchester	1885–1886	Nov.	27	1890	55	6	23
Hobbs, Frank K.	Ossipee	1893–1894						
Hodgdon, Hiram	Ashland	1879–1880						
Houlston, Arthur L.	Ossipee	1891–1892						
Hoit, Nathan	Moultonborough	1797–8–9	Jan.	9	1820	75		
Hoit, Daniel	Sandwich	1820–1–2–8	Aug.	11	1859	80	9	16
Hoit, Abraham P.	Bridgewater	1850–1851	July	10	1868	71	9	22
Hoitt, Alfred	Lee	1851–1852	Nov.	9	1883	77		29
Holbrook, George	Manchester	1870–1871						
Holman, Charles*	Nashua	1875–1876						
Holt, Hermon	Claremont	1895–1896						
Horn, Nathaniel	Dover	1899–1900						
Hoskins, Timothy*	Westmoreland	1843–1844	Aug.		1857			
Howard, Joseph W.	Nashua	1893–1894						
Howard, Timothy J.	Manchester	1897–1898						
Hubbard, John	Charlestown	1789						
Hunt, Israel, Jr.	Nashua	1834–5–6	Sept.	10	1866	54	6	16
Huntington, Ziba	Lebanon	1821–1822	Jan.	15	1858	80 74		

STATE SENATORS FROM 1784 TO 1900. 17

Huntington, Newton S.	Hanover	1883–1884	Oct.	29	1870	73		
Hurd, Ezekiel	Dover	1857–1858	Aug.	30	1821	49	2	21
Jackson, Levi	Chesterfield	1812–13–14–15	Oct.	12	1876	93	2	21
Jackson, Eleazer, Jr.	Cornish	1820–1–2						
Jameson, Thomas G.	Somersworth	1885–1886						
Jameson, Nathan C.	Antrim	1887–1888						
Jenness, Richard	Deerfield	1862–5–8	July	4	1819	73	2	18
Jenness, Benjamin	Deerfield	1857–1858	Jan.	23	1871	82	1	
Jenness, Richard*	Portsmouth	1849–1850	Feb.	2	1872	70		
Jenness, David	Rye	1857–1888						
Jewett, Frederick	Claremont	1899–1900						
Jewett, Stephen S.	Laconia	1899–1900						
Johnson, Stephen	Walpole	1825–1826	Jan.	29	1836	68	3	9
Johnson, James H.	Bath	1839–1840	Sept.	12	1887	84	8	17
Johnson, Simeon B.	Littleton	1841	Sept.	11	1839	73	9	24
Johnson, James W.	Enfield	1876–1877	Dec.	18	1886	60	9	
Jones, Samuel*	Bradford	1834–7–8	Feb.	12	1866	80		
Jordan, George	Warner	1871–1872						
Jordan, Ichabod G.	Somersworth	1853–1854	Feb.	21	1873	66	4	16
Jordan, Chester B*	Lancaster	1897–1898						
Kaley, Timothy	Milford	1881–1882	Sept.	17	1882	65	3	26
Kent, William A.	Concord	1869–13–14	April	7	1840	73	9	18
Kent, Amos	Chester	1814–1815	June	18	1824	49		
Kent, Henry O.	Lancaster	1885–1886						
Kennard, Joseph F.	Manchester	1868–1869	Nov.	7	1892	65	7	25
Kennett, A. Crosby	Conway	1897–1898						
Kenrick, Charles C.	Franklin	1897–1898						
Killoren, Andrew	Dover	1893–1894						
Kimball, Daniel	Plainfield	1804–5–6–12–13	Feb.	27	1817	62		
Kimball, John*	Exeter	1822–3–4	Nov.		1849	79		
Kimball, John*	Concord	1881–1882						
Kingsbury, Sanford	Claremont	1790–1791	Nov.	12	1835	70	1	6
Kingsbury, Nathaniel	Temple	1846	March	3	1870	71	8	6
Knight, William F.	Laconia	1895–1896						
Knowlton, Nathaniel	Hopkinton	1831–1832	July	13	1835	53		
Laighton, John	Portsmouth	1883–1884			1841	50		
Lamprey, Smith	Kensington	1825–1836			1836			

Name.	Residence.	Service.	Died.		Year.	Age.	Mos.	Days.
Langdon, Woodbury*	Portsmouth	1784	Jan.	13	1805	66		
Langdon, John	Portsmouth	1784	Sept.	18	1819	78	2	24
Langdon, John, Jr.	Portsmouth	1818	May	25	1852	47	4	5
Langdon, Francis E.	Portsmouth	1887–1888	Feb.	4	1890	45	2	26
Lane, Charles	Meredith	1845–1847	Jan.	6	1876	58	3	
Lang, George W.	Hebron	1827–1828	Aug.	5	1877	83	10	
Langley, Jeremiah	Durham	1865–1866						
Learnard, Silas F.	Chester	1881–1882	Aug.	4	1880	73	6	4
Leavitt, Moses	North Hampton	1794–5–6–7–8–9, 1800.	Sept.	1	1863	60		
Leavitt, Thomas	Exeter	1876						1
Leighton, Thomas B	Portsmouth	1857–1839	May	18	1866	61		
Liscom, Lemuel F.	Hinsdale	1857–1858						6
Livermore, Arthur	Holderness	1821–1822	July	1	1853	86	11	10
Livingston, Jonas	Peterborough	1869	Nov.	23	1877	70	11	
Long, Peirce	Portsmouth	1788	April	3	1789	50		
Long, George	Portsmouth	1819–1820	April	8	1845	87		
Looney, Charles H.	Milton	1887–1888						
Lord, Jotham, Jr.	Westmoreland	1821–1822	Feb.	17	1843	55	8	16
Lovell, Warren	Meredith	1833–1834	Aug.	18	1875	72		
Lyman, John D.	Exeter	1859–60 1883–4						
Mann, Edward F.	Benton	1879–80–1–2	Aug.	19	1892	46	11	13
March, Jonas C	Rochester	1813–14–15	Aug.	20	1820	36		
Marcy, Daniel	Portsmouth	1864–5–71	Nov.	3	1893	83	11	25
Marshall, Samuel	Derry	1849–1850	Dec.	10	1882	90	10	20
Marshall, Thomas H	Mason	1867–1868	Dec.	16	1872	68		15
Martin, Noah	Dover	1835–1836	May	28	1863	61	10	3
Martin, Samuel H.	Manchester	1875						
Mason, Larkin D.	Tamworth	1855	Jan.	29	1892	74	1	16
Mason, William H. H.	Moultonborough	1864–1865						
Maynard, Frank W.	Nashua	1899–1900						
McClary, Michael	Epsom	1796–7–8–9–1800–1801	March	24	1824	71		
McClary, John*	Epsom	1784–5–6	June	16	1801	82		
McClary, James H.	Epsom	1862	July	11	1810	45		

STATE SENATORS FROM 1784 TO 1900.

McClary, John	Epsom	1819	Dec.	12	1821		
McDaniel, George	Barrington	1841–1842	April	7	1871		
McDuffee, John	Rochester	1786–9 1795–6 1801–1802	Oct.	15	1817	3	16
McGaffey, Neal	Sandwich	1857–1858	Nov.	30	1852		
McGregor, James	Londonderry	1783	Aug.	23	1818		
McKean, William	Deering	1844–1845	June	19	1849		4
McKean, Albert	Nashua	1851	Oct.	30	1887		
McLane, John*	Milford	1891-2-3-4					
Means, Robert	Amherst	1787-9-91	Jan.	24	1823		26
Means, Charles T	Manchester	1889–1890					
Melvin, Nathaniel P	Bridgewater	1837–1838	Oct.	17	1855		18
Melvin, Thomas J.*	Chester	1855–1856	Jan.	29	1881	9	5
Merrill, Abel	Warren	1820	March	26	1858	9	
Merrill, Thomas	Enfield	1852–1853	May	25	1863	4	8
Merrill, Sherburne R	Colebrook	1879–80–1–2	April	9	1891	9	
Miller, Elijah	Hanover	1829–1830	Jan.	10	1857	3	
Miller, George E	Pembroke	1899–1900					
Minot, James	Bristol	1827	Feb.	29	1864		26
Mitchell, William H	Littleton	1889–1890					
Monroe, Hiram	Hillsborough	1849–1850	May	28	1871	7	4
Montgomery, Samuel P	Strafford	1849–1850	Nov.	8	1885	21	
Mooney, John	Meredith	1800	Oct.	8	1826		
Moore, Humphrey	Milford	1841	April	8	1871	5	20
Moore, Orren C	Nashua	1879–1880	May	12	1888	9	3
Moore, Joseph C	Gilford	1881–1882	Jan.	26	1849	7	19
Morril, David L.*	Goffstown	1823	July	28	1836	10	12
Morrill, Ezekiel	Canterbury	1823–1824	April	9	1870	8	26
Morrill, Jonathan	Brentwood	1843–1844	April	6	1893		
Morrill, David, Jr	Canterbury	1860–1861					
Morrison, Leonard A	Windham	1887–1888					
Morse, Charles A	Newmarket	1899–1900	Jan.	8	1892	4	29
Morse, John W	Bradford	1865–1866					
Morton, William H	Rollinsford	1885–1886					
Moses, Thaddeus S	Meredith	1889–1890	July	23	1894		
Moulton, John C	Laconia	1871–1872	March	10	1879	7	23
Mudgett, Nathan	Newport	1855–1856	April	14	1884		22
Mugridge, John Y.*	Concord	1868–1869					

Name.	Residence.	Service.	Died.	Year.	Age.	Mos.	Days.
Murry, Samuel F.	Wilton	1895–1896.					
Musgrove, Richard W.	Bristol	1891–1892.					
Nealley, Benjamin F.	Dover	1887–1888.					
Nettleton, Jeremiah D.	Newport	1840–1841.	Dec. 8	1852	58	6	29
Newcomb, Daniel	Keene	1795–1800–5.	July 14	1818	71	2	26
Newell, Joseph	Wilton	1865–1866.	Feb. 17	1881	87		
Noyes, Oliver H.	Henniker	1877.					
Nute, Alonzo	Farmington	1867–1868.	Dec. 24	1892	66	10	13
Nute, John H.	Dover	1889–1890.					
Nutter, George	Barnstead	1839–1840.					
Nye, Jonathan	Claremont	1827.	Jan. 23	1861	63		1
Olcott, Simeon	Charlestown	1784.	April 1	1843	62	4	27
Olzendam, Abraham P.	Manchester	1885–1886.	Feb. 25	1895	73	2	21
Ordway, John	Hampstead	1857–1858.	Dec. 25	1896	75	3	14
Ordway, Nehemiah G.	Warner	1879–1880.	Nov. 8	1891	89		25
Orr, John	Bedford	1797–8–9, 1890–1–2–3–4–5.					
Page, William	Charlestown	1791.	Jan. 14	1823	75	11	25
Page, Asa	Sutton	1846–1847.	Feb. 2	1810	60	11	14
Page, Calvin	Portsmouth	1893–1894.	July	1885	85		
Paige, Daniel	Weare	1857–1858.	Feb. 1	1875	76	3	5
Paine, Samuel E.	Berlin	1887–1888.					
Palmer, Henry H.	Piermont	1895–1896.					
Parker, James	Litchfield	1819.	May 26	1822	48	1	10
Parker, Asa	Jaffrey	1826–1827.	Oct. 15	1833	45	8	
Parker, Nahum *	Fitzwilliam	1828.	Nov. 12	1839	79		8
Parker, James U.*	Merrimack	1846.	March 21	1871	73		
Parker, Nathan	{ Bedford and Manchester }	1854–1855.	May 7	1894	85	5	17
Parker, John M.	Goffstown	1858–1859.					
Parker, William T.*	Merrimack	1866–1867.	Nov. 30	1884	72		21
Parker, Eleazer B.	Franconia	1873–1874.	May 12	1884	65	5	3
Parker, John M.	Fitzwilliam	1881–1882.					
Parrott, John F.	Portsmouth	1830.	July 9	1836	68		

STATE SENATORS FROM 1784 TO 1900.

Name	Town	Years	Month	Day	Year		
Parsons, John W	Rye	1826-7-8	Sept.	7	1849		
Parsons, Thomas J	Rye	1855-1856	March	28	1880	2	4
Pattee, John	Goffstown	1824	March	15	1829	6	15
Patten, David	Hancock	1845-1846	May	5	1873	5	
Patten, William C	Kingston	1861-1862	Jan.	20	1873	4	
Payne, Elisha	Lebanon	1786-1787	July	20	1807	10	
Payson, Seth	Rindge	1802-1804	Feb.	30	1820		21
Payson, Moses P.*	Bath	1804-5-7-8-9, 1813-14-15	Oct.	7	1828		22
Peabody, Nathaniel	Atkinson	1785-90-1-2	June	3	1823	11	
Peabody, Oliver*	Exeter	1790-3-4, 1813	Aug.		1831		2
Pearson, John C	Boscawen	1889-1890					
Pease, Zebulon	Freedom	1843-1844					
Pease, Elwin	Conway	1868	Aug.	31	1863	4	9
Peavey, George C	Strafford	1869-1870	May	5	1879	3	20
Peavey, George S	Greenfield	1893-1894			1876		
Peirce, Ezra L	Westmoreland	1802-1803	Sept.	16	1868		
Penhallow, Hunking	Portsmouth	1821	Sept.	24	1826	3	8
Perley, John L	Meredith	1841-1842	Sept.	18	1888	2	20
Perkins, Orren	Winchester	1865-1866	Oct.	30	1880		
Perkins, Benjamin F	Bristol	1883-1884					
Perkins, Nathan R	Jefferson	1889-1890					
Perry, William G	Manchester	1879-1880	Nov.	29	1887	3	4
Philbrick, Emmons B	Rye	1878-9-80					
Pickering, John*	Portsmouth	1788-1789	April	11	1805	6	20
Pickering, James	Newington	1840-1841	July	13	1855		
Pierce, Andrew	Dover	1825-1826	March	29	1850	4	19
Pierce, Andrew, Jr	Dover	1843	Dec.	19	1891	1	
Pierce, Frederick B	Chesterfield	1899-1900					
Pierce, Thomas P	Nashua	1874	Oct.	14	1887	1	14
Pierce, George W	Winchester	1891-1892					
Pike, Austin F.*	Franklin	1857-1858	Oct.	8	1886	4	10
Pike, Chester*	Cornish	1883-4-5-6	Nov.	29	1897	2	29
Pindar, Joseph D	Newmarket	1848	May	12	1875	6	26
Pitman, Joseph	Bartlett	1851	Oct.	23	1857		
Pitman, George W. M.*	Bartlett	1870-1871	Dec.	3	1898		
Pitman, Lycurgus	Conway	1887-1888					
Pitts, Albert	Charlestown	1879-1880	Dec.	19	1898	8	25

Names.	Residence.	Service.	Died.		Year.	Age.	Mos.	Days.
Plumer, Beard	Milton	1809-10-11-12-16	Oct.	7	1816	62		
Plumer, William *	Epping	1810-1811	Dec.	23	1850	91	5	29
Plumer, William, Jr	Epping	1827-1828	Sept.	18	1854	65	6	20
Poole, Benjamin	Hollis	1817-18-19-20	April	20	1836	65	3	4
Poole, James	Hanover	1823	July	18	1828	42		
Porter, Reuben	Sutton	1834-1835	Aug.	3	1879	89		2
Porter, Royal H	Keene	1876-1877						
Poor, Noyes	Goffstown	1847-1848	July	6	1855	60		16
Prentiss, John	Keene	1838-1839	June	6	1873	95	9	
Prescott, William	Gilmanton	1827	Oct.	18	1875	86	10	20
Preston, John	New Ipswich	1848-1849	March	5	1867	64		24
Preston, George C	Henniker	1883-1894						
Priest, James	Derry	1874-1875	June	28	1882	79	2	21
Proctor, David E	Wilton	1889-1900						
Proctor, John	Andover	1875	Dec.	30	1883	79	4	18
Putney, Walter	Bow							
Quarles, Samuel	Ossipee	1810-11-12	July	7	1846	79		13
Quincy, Josiah *	Rumney	1841-1842	Jan.	19	1875	81	10	
Quinby, Henry B	Gilford	1889-1890						
Read, Benjamin	Swanzey	1867-1868						
Reed, William J	Westmoreland	1895-1896						
Renton, Peter	Concord	1840-1841	Feb.	15	1865	82		
Reynolds, Leonard P	Manchester	1893-1894						
Richardson, Samuel M	Pelham	1821	March	11	1858	79		
Richards, Dexter	Newport	1887-1888	Aug.	7	1888		11	3
Richards, Seth M	Newport	1897-1898						
Rixford, William H	Concord	1855	July	31	1890	79	6	24
Rix, James M.*	Lancaster	1852-1853	March	25	1856	44		
Robb, John	Acworth	1848-1849	May	26	1855	63		
Robinson, Terley	Poplin	1845						
Robinson, Isaiah L	Fremont	1867-1868						
Robinson, Henry	Concord	1883-1884						
Rogers, Nathaniel	Newmarket	1789-90-1	May,		1829	83		

STATE SENATORS FROM 1784 TO 1900.

Name	Town	Years			1879	85	9	19
Rollins, William W.	Somersworth	1846		Dec.	3			
Rollins, Frank M.	Gilford	1887–1888						
Rollins, Amos L.	Alton	1895–1896						
Rollins, Frank W.*	Concord	1895–1896				81	11	
Rowell, Charles	Allenstown	1856–1857		Jan.	11	1867		
Rowe, George R.	Brentwood	1891–1892						
Rugg, Daniel W.	Sullivan	1889–1890						
Russell, Moore	Plymouth	1801–2–3, 1810–11–12		August	14	1838	95	16
Rust, Henry B.	Wolfeborough	1830–1831		July	27	1876	82	
Safford, James F.	Farmington	1899–1900						
Sanborn, Josiah	Epsom	1810–11–12		June	14	1842	78	14
Sanborn, Charles	East Kingston	1849–1850		March	1	1882	73	13
Sanborn, Henry F.	Epsom	1866–1867		March	26	1897	78	1
Sanborn, Charles	Sandown	1873						
Sanborn, John L.	Manchester	1899–1900						
Sanborn, John W.*	Wakefield	1874–1875						
Sargent, Jonathan E.*	Wentworth	1854		Jan.	6	1890	73	2
Sawyer, Aaron W.	Nashua	1855–1858		Aug.	23	1882	63	10
Sawyer, Oliver D.	Weare	1887–1888						
Scammon, Richard M.	Stratham	1891–1892						
Scott, Charles	Peterborough	1897–1898						
Scripture, Gilman	Nashua	1863–1870		Nov.	26	1887	73	13
Seavey, James F.	Dover	1881–2–3–4						22
Shannon, Nathaniel	Moultonborough	1865–6–7–8–17–18		July	27	1826	72	28
Shannon, John S.	Gilmanton	1851–1852		Aug.	4	1868	36	20
Shaw, Tristram	Hampton	1834		March	14	1843	69	
Shaw, Albert M.	Lebanon	1878–9–80		Jan.	31	1889	74	
Sheafe, James	Portsmouth	1791–2–9		Dec.	6	1829		
Shepard, Amos*	Alstead	{1786–7–8–9–90–2–5–6– 7–8–9–1800–1–2–3}		Jan.	1	1812	65	
Shepard, Samuel	Gilmanton	1809–1813		Nov.	16	1836	76	
Shepard, Joseph	Epping	1816		Nov.	9	1845	76	
Shepard, William H	Derry	1879–1880		April	9	1833		22
Sinclair, John G.	Bethlehem	1858–1859						
Sinclair, Charles A.	Portsmouth	1889–90–1–2–5–6						
Sinclair, William C.	Ossipee	1885–1886		May	28	1875	80	
Slader, Jesse	Acworth	1859–1860						

Names.	Residence.	Service.	Died.		Year.	Age.	Mos.	Days.
Slayton, Hiram K	Manchester	1877–1878	July	9	1896	70	10	21
Sleeper, Jonas D	Haverhill	1854–1855	Sept.	9	1868	53	5	
Small, William B	Newmarket	1870	April	7	1878	60	10	21
Smith, Ebenezer*	Meredith	1784–7–8–9–90–2–3–4–5–6	Aug.	22	1807	73		
Smith, Jedediah K	Amherst	1804–5–6–9	Dec.	17	1828	58	7	10
Smith, James	Grantham	1826	Oct.	24	1843	76		
Smith, Daniel M	Lempster	1842–1843	March	9	1872	75	11	14
Smith, Joseph H	Dover	1844–1845	Feb.	25	1886	80		11
Smith, Isaac W	Manchester	1862–1863	Nov.	28	1898	73	6	
Smith, Charles J	Mont Vernon	1863–1864						
Smith, Thomas J	Wentworth	1866–1867	May	1	1892	62		14
Smith, Alvah	Lempster	1871	Aug.	7	1879	82	6	21
Smith, Joshua B	Durham	1875–1876						
Smith, Charles E	Dover	1879–1880						
Smith, George S	Charlestown	1891–1892						
Snow, Edwin	Eaton	1891–1892						
Spalding, John A	Nashua	1878						
Stark, Frederick G	Manchester	1830–1831	March	29	1861	68	8	4
Stark, Caleb	Dunbarton	1818	Aug.	26	1838	78		
Stark, Charles	Manchester	1853	Aug.	19	1873	72		
Stearns, Onslow*	Concord	1862–1863	Dec.	29	1878	68	4	
Stearns, Ezra S	Rindge	1887–8–9–90						
Stearns, George H	Manchester	1889–1890						
Steel, David	Goffstown	1828–1829	Oct.	1	1875	79	10	
Stevens, Ezra A*	Portsmouth	1867–1868						
Stevens, Lyman D	Concord	1885–1886						
Stevens, Charles W	Nashua	1895–1896						
Stiles, David	Lyndeborough	1837	June	24	1870	90	6	3
Storer, Clement*	Portsmouth	1803–4–5–6–17	Nov.	21	1830	70		
Stowell, George H	Claremont	1874–1875						
Straw, Jacob	Henniker	1841–1842	Sept.	12	1856	64	9	24
Straw, Ezekiel A*	Manchester	1864–1865	Oct.	23	1882	62	7	16
Sullivan, George	Exeter	1814–1815	April	14	1838	66		

STATE SENATORS FROM 1784 TO 1900.

Name	Town	Dates	Month	Day	Year	Age		
Sullivan, Miah B	Dover	1891–1892						
Sulloway, Alvah W	Franklin	1891–1892						
Swett, Joseph	Andover	1843–1844						
Symmes, Ebenezer	Concord	1853–1854	Jan.	25	1878	83		22
Taggart, David A.*	Goffstown	1889–1890	Jan.	7	1881	87	4	22
Talpey, Charles W	Farmington	1881–1882						
Tallant, John G	Concord	1891–1892						
Tasker, John C	Dover	1893–1894						
Taylor, Timothy†	Merrimack	1796						
Taylor, Nathan	Sanbornton	1799–1800–1–2–3–4	April		1840	84	3	15
Taylor, Andrew	Canterbury	1846	Dec.	27	1862	73	10	28
Taylor, Jacob	Stoddard	1851–1852	Dec.	7	1895	98	4	29
Taylor, Cyrus	Bristol	1869–1870	May	16	1898	79		
Taylor, Matthew H	Salem	1871–1872						
Taylor, Jonathan M	Sanbornton	1883–1884						
Taylor, John F	Tilton	1885–1886	Nov.	23	1887	58	5	22
Tennant, James B	Epsom	1889–1890						
Tenney, Ralph E	Hollis	1847–1848	Oct.	19	1854	64	5	15
Thompson, Ebenezer	Durham	1787	Aug.	14	1802	65		10
Thornton, Matthew	Merrimack	1784–5–6	June	24	1803	89		
Thurston, Frank G	Nashua	1885–1886						
Todd, George E	Concord	1874–1876	Nov.	16	1892	62	9	11
Todd, George W	Mont Vernon	1879–1880	April	18	1884	55	5	
Toppan, Christopher	Hampton	1788–9–91–2–3	Feb.	18	1818	83	1	10
Towle, George S.*	Lebanon	1859–1860	Dec.	19	1882	67	5	17
Towle, George H	Deerfield	1881–1882						
Towle, Frank C	Hooksett	1895–1896	Sept.	30	1895	48	4	1
Treadwell, Thomas P	Portsmouth	1842	Nov.	5	1878	73	1	11
Treat, John S	Portsmouth	1881–1882	March	8	1898	60	6	27
Truesdell, Edmund E	Pembroke	1887–1888						
Tufts, Charles A	Dover	1861–1862						
Tuttle, Jacob	Antrim	1833	Aug.	20	1848	81	6	15
Tuttle, Bradbury C	Meredith	1852–1853	Nov.	24	1885	76		
Tyler, Austin	Claremont	1838	Aug.	12	1844	54	7	7
Upham, George B	Claremont	1814	Feb.	10	1848	79	1	14
Van Dyke, Thomas H	Stewartstown	1895–1896						
Varney, David B	Manchester	1881–1882						

† Deceased; date of death unknown.

26   NEW HAMPSHIRE MANUAL.

Names.	Residence.	Service.	Died.		Year.	Age.	Mos.	Days.
Vaughan, Orsino A. J.	Laconia	1866–1867						
Vose, Roger	Walpole	1869–10–12	April	30	1876	57	1	20
Vose, John	Atkinson	1816	April	17	1842	79	1	24
Vose, Frederick	Walpole	1847–1848	April	3	1840	73	9	24
Wadleigh, John	Meredith	1862–1863	Nov.		1871	70		
Wallace, Robert	Henniker	1788–9–90–1–2	Oct.	25	1873	67		
Wallace, James	Milford	1814–15–16	Jan.	30	1815	65		
Wallace, John, Jr.	Milford	1821–2–3–4–8	July	3	1828	63		
Wallace, Edwin	Rochester	1873	Aug.	4	1837	56		
Wallace, Albert	Rochester	1897–1898	Oct.	29	1894	71	9	25
Waldron, John	Dover	1788–90–1–2–4–1803–4–5–6	Aug.	31	1827	87	10	10
Walker, Timothy	Concord	1784	May	5	1822	84	10	10
Walker, Joseph B.	Concord	1893–1894						
Warde, David A.*	Concord	1872–1873	May	14	1874	46	3	14
Warner, Simeon	Whitefield	1842–1843	Nov.	29	1880	93	5	
Wason, George A.	New Boston	1883–4–95–6						
Waterhouse, William E.	Barrington	1893–1894						
Weare, John M.	Seabrook	1853–1854						
Webster, Ebenezer	Salisbury	1785–6–8–90	April	6	1806	67		
Webster, Ezekiel	Boscawen	1815	April	10	1829	49	1	
Webster, Stephen P.	Haverhill	1823–4–5			1841			
Webster, Robert S.	Barnstead	1857–1858						
Weeks, Amos	Nashua	1883–1884						
Weeks, John W.	Lancaster	1826–7–8	July	18	1853	74	5	17
Weeks, William P.*	Canaan	1848–1849	Jan.	8	1870	66	10	5
Weeks, Joseph D.	Canaan	1875–1878	Dec.	1	1890	53	1	14
Wells, John S.*	Exeter	1851–1852	Aug.	1	1860	56	9	
Welch, John T.	Dover	1897–1898						
Wentworth, John	Dover	1784–1785	Jan.	10	1787	41	5	24
Wentworth, Joshua	Portsmouth	1785–6–7–8	Oct.	19	1809	68	9	16
Wentworth, Ezekiel	Ossipee	1829–1830	April	4	1852	68	11	12
Wentworth, Eli	Milton	1860–1861	July	18	1863	42	5	
Wentworth, Nathaniel	Hudson	1897–1898						

STATE SENATORS FROM 1784 TO 1900. 27

Wheeler, John W	Salem	1877-1878					
Wheeler, Benjamin R	Salem	1883-1884					
White, William	Chester	1806-7-8					
White, Daniel M	Peterborough	1878	Nov.	9	1829		
Whitcomb, Elisha	Swanzey	1793-4-6-7-8-9-1800-1	Sept.	17	1814		
Whitehouse, Charles S	Rochester	1863-1864					72
Whitaker, John	Concord	1893-1894					
Whittemore, Aaron	Pembroke	1831-1832	April		1850		75
Whittemore, Bernard B	Nashua	1852-1853	March	5	1863	9	75
Whittemore, Amos	Bennington	1870	April	18	1881	1	70
Whittemore, Aaron, Jr	Pittsfield	1883-1884	May	4	1885		30
Whittemore, Jacob B	Hillsborough	1891-1892					
Whitney, George A	Rindge	1875					
Wiggin, Samuel B	Sandwich	1897-1898					
Willard, Lockhart	Keene	1806-7-8-9-10	March	22	1818	7	55
Willard, David E	Orford	1883-1884	Jan.	17	1895		66
Willard, Isaac	Orford	1889-1890					
Wilcox, Uriah	Newport	1818-1819	March	18	1838	8	73 21 16 15 6
Wild, Nathan	Chesterfield	1833-1834	March	5	1838		50
Wilder, Josiah	Rindge	1811	April		1812		41
Williams, Jared W.*	Lancaster	1832-3-4	Sept.	29	1864	9	65 27
Williamson, Alonzo B	Claremont	1852-1853	March	19	1860	3	44
Wilkins, James McK*	Bedford	1828-1829	Jan.	18	1855	1	70
Willson, Edward T	Farmington	1882-1880					
Woodbury, Peter	Francestown	1832-1833	Sept.	12	1834	8	67
Woodbury, John*	Salem	1836-1837	Feb.	5	1849		65 4
Woodbury, Peter P	Bedford	1851-1852	Dec.	5	1860		69
Woodbury, Edward B	Manchester	1885-1886					
Woodbury, Frank P	Salem	1891-1892					
Wood, John	Keene	1819-1823	Oct.	6	1856		78
Woods, Edward	Bath	1893-1894					
Woodward, Clement J	Keene	1883-1884					
Woolson, Thomas	Claremont	1828	July	3	1837		60
Worcester, Francis	Plymouth	1787-1788	Oct.	19	1802	11	81 4
Worcester, Franklin	Hollis	1887-1888					
Yeaton, Henry A	Portsmouth	1899-1900					83
Young, Dan	Lisbon	1816-17-18-19-20	March	28	1867		21

Total members in 117 years, 762.   Deceased members in 115 years, 513.

SUPPLEMENT

TO

State Manual No. 6

New Hampshire Senate.

1784 to 1902.

THE NEW YORK
PUBLIC LIBRARY

ASTOR, LENOX AND
TILDEN FOUNDATIONS
R   1915   L

NEW HAMPSHIRE SENATE.

No. 107.

1901—1902.

DISTRICT.		RESIDENCE.
1.	Twitchell, Cassius M. C.	Milan.
2.	Remich, Daniel C.	Littleton.
3.	Chase, Ira A.	Bristol.
4.	Bean, Edwin C.	Belmont.
5.	Farnham, J. Frank	Wakefield.
6.	Leach, Edward G.	Franklin.
7.	Brooks, Nathaniel G.	Charlestown.
8.	Farnum, Edwin W. H.	Francestown.
9.	Head, Eugene S.	Hooksett.
10.	Stevens, Henry W.	Concord.
11.	Little, George P.	Pembroke.
12.	Locke, James A.	Somersworth.
13.	Ellis, Bertram	Keene.
14.	Annett, Albert	Jaffrey.
15.	Kaley, Frank E.	Milford.
16.	Ray, Harry P.	Manchester.
17.	Shontell, Frederick W.	Manchester.
18.	Sullivan, Michael F.	Manchester.
19.	Pillsbury, William S.	Londonderry.
20.	Jones, Andros B.	Nashua.
21.	Wetherell, Albert S.	Exeter.
22.	Bunker, James A.	Rollinsford.
23.	Leddy, John	Epping.
24.	Urch, David	Portsmouth.

Bertram Ellis, President.

PASSED ON.

		Year.	Age.	Months.	Days.
Hatch, John K.	April 10,	1861	76	3	23
Robinson, Perley	Nov. 13,	1888	87	7	22
Weare, John M.	Dec. 21,	1898	84	7	17
Webster, Robert S.	Jan. 17,	1899	78	2	15
Tufts, Charles A.	Feb. 12,	1899	77	3	7
Whitehouse, Charles S.	Mar. 4,	1899	71	6	2
Barton, Levi W.	Mar. 10,	1899	81	0	10
Sinclair, Charles A.	Apr. 22,	1899	50	8	2
Clarke, Nathaniel H.	Apr. 27,	1899	73	2	2
Sinclair, John G.	June 27,	1899	73	3	3
Huntington, Newton S.	Aug. 2,	1899	76	11	24
Davis, Walter S.	Nov. 1,	1899	65	3	4
Reynolds, Leonard P.	Dec. 20,	1899	47	3	9
Bartlett, Charles H.	Jan. 25,	1900	66	3	11
Rollins, Amos L.	Feb. 22,	1900	73	2	12
Balcom, George L.	May 13,	1900	80	7	5
Taylor, Jonathan M.	May 31,	1900	77	8	11
Cox, Alfred A.	June 21,	1900	74	7	17
Ashley, Horace S.	July 17,	1900	60	7	23
Perkins, Nathan R.	July 26,	1900	71	7	14
Amidon, Charles J.	Aug. 21,	1900	73	3	29
Bingham, Harry	Sept. 12,	1900	79	5	13

Average age of the twenty who have died in the last two years, 71 years, 10 months, 6 days.

GEORGE C. GILMORE.

MANCHESTER, N. H.,
January 3, 1901.

Insert after page 28.

SUPPLEMENT NO. 2

TO

STATE MANUAL NO. 6

NEW HAMPSHIRE SENATE

FROM

1784 TO 1904.

NEW HAMPSHIRE SENATE.

No. 108.

1903—1904.

DISTRICT.		RESIDENCE.
1.	Allen, William F.	Stewartstown.
2.	Keyes, Henry W.	Haverhill.
3.	Whitney, George E.	Enfield.
4.	Lewando, Joseph.	Wolfeborough.
5.	Burnell, Alvah W.	Bartlett.
6.	Tilton, Elmer S.	Laconia.
7.	Cooper, John B.	Newport.
8.	Marvin, Fred J.	Alstead.
9.	Felt, Marcellus H.	Hillsborough.
10.	Stillings, Ferdinand A.	Concord.
11.	Fellows, James G.	Pembroke.
12.	Neal, John H.	Rochester.
13.	Fuller, Levi A.	Marlborough.
14.	Ripley, Franklin.	Troy.
15.	Wilkins, Aaron M.	Amherst.
16.	Lightbody, James.	Manchester.
17.	Bickford, John C.	Manchester.
18.	Foley, Thomas J.	Manchester.
19.	Hoitt, Charles W.	Nashua.
20.	Tolles, Jason E.	Nashua.
21.	Hoyt, Arthur E.	Plaistow.
22.	Thompson, Lucien.	Durham.
23.	Richmond, Allen D.	Dover.
24.	Page, Calvin.	Portsmouth.

Charles W. Hoitt, *President.*

PASSED ON.

			Year.	Age.	Months.	Days.
Clarke, Frank G.	Jan.	9,	1901	50	4	0
Gilman, Edward H.	March	19,	1901	45	10	7
Varney, David B.	March	25,	1901	78	6	29
Moses, Thaddeus S.	Jan.	13,	1902	66	11	16
Means, Charles T.	Jan.	25,	1902	47	0	6
Looney, Charles H.	April	23,	1902	52	9	13
Lyman, John D.	July	31,	1902	79	0	29
Parker, John M.	Sept.	20,	1902	80	0	4
Philbrick, Emmons B.	Oct.	16,	1902	68	11	3
Waterhouse, William E.	Nov.	29,	1902	57	9	29
Morrison, Leonard A.	Dec.	14,	1902	59	9	24

Average age of the eleven who have passed on, in the last two years, 62 years, 5 months, 20 days. Number of Senators from 1784 to 1904, 121 years, 1,460. Number of different men Senators, 809. Amos Shepard was a Senator fifteen years. Passed on, in 119 years, 546.

GEORGE C. GILMORE.

MANCHESTER, N. H.,
January 8, 1903.

Insert after page 28.

SUPPLEMENT NO. 3.

TO

STATE MANUAL NO. 6

NEW HAMPSHIRE SENATE

FROM

1784 TO 1906.

NEW HAMPSHIRE SENATE.

No. 109.

1905—1906.

DISTRICT.		RESIDENCE.
1.	Magoon, Garvin R.	Stratford.
2.	Bell, Ernest L.	Woodstock.
3.	Whitney, George E.	Enfield.
4.	Adams, George H.	Plymouth.
5.	Parker, Samuel S.	Farmington.
6.	Holmes, Frederick A.	Franklin.
7.	Bartlett, George H.	Sunapee.
8.	Kimball, Fred H.	Bennington.
9.	Quimby, Frank P.	Concord.
10.	Dudley, Harry H.	Concord.
11.	Durell, Newman	Pittsfield.
12.	Kelsey, James H.	Nottingham.
13.	Follansbee, George H.	Keene.
14.	Learned, Henry D.	Dublin.
15.	Taft, Herbert J.	Greenville.
16.	Cavanaugh, John B.	Manchester.
17.	Graf, Johann Adam	Manchester.
18.	Dinsmore, Arthur W.	Manchester.
19.	Abbott, Charles W.	Derry.
20.	Cole, Wallace W.	Salem.
21.	Allen, Walter A.	Hampstead.
22.	Clark, Frank B.	Dover.
23.	Loughlin, Thomas	Portsmouth.
24.	Entwistle, Thomas	Portsmouth.

George H. Adams, *President.*

PASSED ON.

Name.	Residence.	Year.	Date.		Age.	Months.	Days.
Whitaker, John	Concord	1903	Jan.	20	67	7	12
Gilman, Virgil C.	Nashua	1903	April	28	75	11	24
Mason, Larkin D.	Tamworth	1903	May	2	93	0	17
Martin, Samuel H.	Manchester	1903	June	16	72	0	0
Sanborn, John W.	Wakefield	1903	July	9	81	5	24
Whittemore, Jacob B.	Hillsborough	1903	Aug.	18	51	8	10
Kenrick, Charles C.	Franklin	1903	Oct.	6	59	5	29
Stevens, Ezra A.	Portsmouth	1903	Nov.	24	76	8	13
Palmer, Henry H.	Piermont	1904	Jan.	5	80	5	5
Cogswell, Thomas	Gilmanton	1904	Feb.	15	63	0	8
Danforth, Charles C.	Concord	1904	March	7	72	10	26
Hatch, John	Greenland	1904	March	16	55	2	16
Morton, William H.	Rollinsford	1904	June	4	90	3	26
Twitchell, Cassius M. C.	Milan	1904	June	9	51	7	28

Average age of the fourteen who have passed on, in the last two years, 70 years 10 months. Number of Senators from 1784 to 1906, 123 years, 1,484. Number of different men Senators, 831.

GEORGE C. GILMORE.

MANCHESTER, N. H.,
January 4, 1905.

Insert after page 28.

NEW HAMPSHIRE MEN AT BUNKER HILL.

Roll of New Hampshire men at the Battle of Bunker Hill, June 17, 1775, their names arranged alphabetically by companies, omitting all who were discharged prior to, or enlisted after that date. Of the twenty-four companies in the battle (including Captain Reuben Dow's) only seven company rolls have been found that give the residences of the men, all the others supplied by the writer from the best information he could obtain from all sources. There were a few men in the New Hampshire companies from Connecticut, Massachusetts, and Vermont.

For volume and page, see New Hampshire State Papers, except where M is placed against the volume and page.

M.—Denotes Massachusetts rolls.

A.—Men in the Arnold expedition to Quebec.

A. P.—Men taken prisoners at Quebec.

*—Men who were paid for loss of equipments and clothing in the Battle of Bunker Hill.

ROLL OF NEW HAMPSHIRE MEN AT BUNKER HILL,
JUNE 17, 1775.

M.—Denotes Massachusetts rolls. A.—Men in the Arnold expedition to Quebec. A. P.—Taken prisoner at Quebec. *.— Men who were paid for loss of equipments and clothing in the battle of Bunker Hill.

Names.	Residence.	Rank.	Company.	Regiment.	Vol.	Page.	Remarks.
Adams, Robert	Londonderry	Private	Reid's	Stark's	14	73	
Alexander, Hugh	"	Lieutenant	"	"	14	73	
Anderson, James	"	Private	"	"	14	73	
Anderson, Matthew	"	"	"	"	14	73	
Anderson, John	"	"	"	"	14	73	
Ayers, Samuel	Pembroke	"	"	"	14	73	
Allen, Josiah *	Concord	Captain	D. Moore's	"	14	215	A. Wounded.
Abbot, Joshua *	"	Sergeant	Abbot's	"	14	60	
Abbot, Jeremiah	"	"	"	"	14	60	
Abbot, Nat. C.	"	Private	"	"	14	60	
Abbot, Stephen	"	"	"	"	14	60	
Abbot, Reuben	"	"	"	"	14	60	
Abbot, Amos	"	"	"	"	14	60	
Aiken, Andrew	Chester	Sergeant	"	"	14	60	Wounded.
Aiken, James	"	Private	"	"	14	60	
Atkinson, Samuel	Boscawen	Lieutenant	Hutchins's	"	14	60	
Abbot, Benjamin	Concord	Sergeant	Kinsman's	"	14	63	
Aiken, James *	Antrim	Private	Woodbury's	"	11	108	
Abbot, Uriah	Pelham	Sergeant	"	"	14	52	
Amy, Heman	Salem	Private	"	"	14	52	
Atwood, Joshua	Pelham	"	"	"	14	52	
Austin, Abiel	Salem	"	"	"	14	52	

NEW HAMPSHIRE MEN AT BUNKER HILL.

Name	Town	Rank	Company	Regiment			Notes
Ahern, Timothy	Goffstown	Private	Richards's	Stark's	14	214	A.
Annis, Samuel	"	"	"	"	14	55	
Allds, John *	Litchfield	"	"	"	14	58	A. P.
Andrews, Anny	Hillsborough	Sergeant	J. Moore's	"	14	50	
Andrews, Anny, Jr.	"	Private	Baldwin's	"	14	50	
Andrews, Isaac	"	"	"	"	14	50	
Adams, David	Gilsum	Sergeant	Stiles's	"	16	37	M.
Archer, Benjamin	Keene	Private	Towne's	"	16	37	M.
Allenwood, Samuel	Amherst	Lieutenant	Hinds's	Reed's	16	48	M.
Aldrich, George *	Westmoreland	Corporal	"	"	14	84	
Aldrich, Caleb	"	Private	"	"	14	84	
Amsden, Thomas	"	"	"	"	14	84	
Archer, Lewis *	New Ipswich	Corporal	Towne's	"	16	32	M.
Adams, Stephen *	"	"	"	"	16	52	M.
Adams, Phinehas	"	Private	"	"	16	52	M.
Adams, Asa	Temple	"	"	"	16	52	M.
Andrews, Jeremiah	"	"	"	"	16	52	M. Died Aug. 7, 1775
Avery, Timothy *	New Ipswich	"	"	"	16	52	A.
Avery, David *	Fitzwilliam	"	Whitcomb's	"	14	92	
Arnold, Edward *	Wilton	"	Walker's	"	14	96	
Abbot, Nathan	Nashua	"	"	"	14	95	
Adams, David	"	"	"	"	14	97	
Adams, David, Jr	"	"	"	"	14	96	
Adams, Richard	Rindge	"	Thomas's	"	14	99	Killed.
Adams, Isaac *	Jaffrey	"	"	"	14	98	
Adams, Stephen *	Walpole	"	"	"	14	99	
Alexander, Richard *	Mason	Corporal	Mann's	"	14	100	
Abbott, Samuel *	"	Private	"	"	14	100	
Adams, John *	"	Sergeant	"	"	14	100	
Allen, Abijah	"	Sergeant	"	"	14	100	
Ames, Simeon *	Amherst	Private	Crosby's	"	14	101	
Averill, Elijah	"	"	Marcy's	"	14	102	
Abbott, Joshua *	"	"	Dow's	"	14	104	
Adams, Daniel *	Hollis	"	"	Prescott's	14	76	M.
Adams, William *	"	"	"	"	56	63	M. A.
Ames, David *							

Names.	Residence.	Rank.	Company.	Regiment.	Vol.	Page.	Remarks.
Abbott, Abraham	New Ipswich	Private	Drury's	Ward's	56	27	M.
Adams, Samuel	Walpole	"	"	"	14	72	M.
Anthony, Joseph	Alstead	"	"	"	14	72	M.
Boyd, William	Manchester	"	Reid's	Stark's	14	74	
Brown, Alexander	Windham	"	"	"	14	73	
Burke, Robert	Londonderry	Drummer	"	"	14	73	
Batchelder, Nathaniel*	Nottingham	Private	Dearborn's	"	14	68	
Berry, Benjamin*	Epsom	"	"	"	14	68	
Beverly, James*	Nottingham	"	"	"	14	215	A. P.
Bickford, Andrew*	"	Corporal	"	"	14	68	
Bickford, John*	Chichester	Private	"	"	14	211	A.
Brown, Nicholas*	Nottingham	"	"	"	14	68	
Baker, Thomas	Pembroke	Sergeant	D. Moore's	"	14	70	
Bartlett, Christopher*	Alexandria	Corporal	"	"	14	70	
Batchelder, Nathan*	Deerfield	"	"	"	14	70	Wounded.
Batchelder, Josiah	"	Private	"	"	14	70	
Blake, Paul*	Epping	"	"	"	14	70	Killed.
Broderick, Joseph	"	"	"	"	14	70	
Brown, Abraham	Epping	"	"	"	14	72	
Brown, Ensley*	Hopkinton	"	"	"	14	70	
Buswell, John*	"	"	"	"	14	70	
Barnes, Amos	Hopkinton	"	Abbot's	"	14	60	
Bowley, John	Boscawen	"	"	"	14	60	
Bradley, Jonathan	Concord	"	"	"	14	61	
Burbank, Moses, Jr	Boscawen	"	"	"	14	60	
Burbank, David	"	"	"	"	14	60	
Burbank, Nathaniel	"	"	"	"	14	60	
Badger, Ezra	Chester	"	Hutchins's	"	14	63	
Baker, Benjamin*	Canterbury	"	"	"	14	63	
Basford, Benjamin	Alexandria	"	"	"	14	64	
Beard, William*	New Boston	"	"	"	14	64	
Bean, Cornelius	Sutton	"	"	"	14	63	
Bean, John	Canterbury	"	"	"	14	210	

NEW HAMPSHIRE MEN AT BUNKER HILL.

Name	Town	Rank	Company	Regiment			
Bean, John, Jr........	Canterbury....	Private......	Hutchins's...	Stark's......	14	65	A.
Boynton, Joshua.....	"	"	"	"	14	65	
Boynton, Edmund....	"	"	"	"	14	211	A.
Bunten, John.........	Allenstown....	"	"	"	14	63	
Burns, James........	New Boston...	"	"	"	14	65	
Burns, John, Jr......	"	"	"	"	14	65	A.
Bean, Ebenezer*.....	Bow..........	"	Kinsman's...	"	14	210	
Bean, George........	Meredith......	"	"	"	14	66	
Bond, Samuel........	"	"	"	"	14	66	
Brown, Josiah.......	Epping........	"	Woodbury's..	"	14	66	
Bailey, Enoch.......	Salem.........	"	"	"	14	215	A.
Barker, Isaac........	Pelham........	"	"	"	14	52	
Bettis, Robert.......	"	"	"	"	14	52	
Blanchard, John.....	Salem.........	"	Richards's...	"	14	52	
Bradford, William...	Bedford.......	"	"	"	14	52	
Barnet, William.....	Goffstown.....	"	"	"	14	55	
Bean, John..........	"	Sergeant.....	"	"	14	55	
Bell, Jonathan.......	"	Corporal.....	"	"	14	55	
Blake, Timothy.....	Goffstown.....	Private......	"	"	14	55	
Blake, Jonathan.....	"	Corporal.....	J. Moore's...	"	14	56	
Blake, Elijah........	Manchester...	Private......	"	"	14	55	
Bradbury, Jacob.....	Merrimack....	"	"	"	14	58	
Butterfield, Peter....	Litchfield.....	Lieutenant...	Baldwin's....	"	14	58	
Baker, Benjamin....	Manchester...	Fifer.........	"	"	14	57	
Barron, Samuel......	Litchfield.....	Captain......	"	"	14	58	
Bixby, Edward*.....	Hillsborough..	Sergeant.....	"	"	14	30	Killed.
Boyd, Nathaniel.....	"	Fifer.........	"	"	14	30	
Butterfield, James...	Hopkinton....	Sergeant.....	"	"	14	50	
Baldwin, Isaac*.....	Hillsborough..	Drummer....	"	"	14	51	
Bailey, Moses.......	"	Private......	Scott's.......	"	14	30	
Blake, Henry.......	Peterborough.	Corporal.....	"	"	16	40	M.
Bradford, Samuel*..	Society.......	Private......	"	"	16	40	M.
Brown, John........							
Brooks, David......							
Bailey, Andrew.....							
Barnard, Jonathan...							

Names.	Residence.	Rank.	Company.	Regiment.	Vol.	Page.	Remarks.
Blair, John	Peterborough	Private	Scott's	Stark's	16	40	M.
Blood, Zacheus	Washington	"	"	"	16	40	M.
Burrows, Nathaniel	Windham	"	"	"	16	40	M.
Baker, John	Walpole	Fifer	Stiles's	"	16	44	M.
Bassett, Samuel	Keene	Private	"	"	16	44	M.
Beckwith, Niles	Lempster	"	"	"	16	44	M.
Bemis, Henry	Nelson	"	"	"	16	44	M.
Billings, Ebenezer	Keene	"	"	"	16	44	M.
Bradley, William	"	"	Towne's	"	16	48	M.
Bailey, Joel	Hollis	"	"	"	16	48	M.
Bailey, Richard	"	"	"	"	16	48	M.
Barrett, Moses	Hudson	Sergeant	"	"	16	48	M.
Blodget, Jacob	Hollis	Private	"	"	16	44	M.
Britton, Samuel	Amherst	"	"	"	16	44	M.
Bruce, Josiah	Hollis	"	"	"	16	44	M.
Burrows, Josiah	Londonderry	"	"	"	16	44	M.
Barker, Abner *	Haverhill	Surgeon		Reed's	7	398	
Bailey, Dudley	Salem	Fifer	Hutchins's	"	14	76	
Bond, Gilbert *	Hampstead	Private	"	"	14	76	
Brown, Samuel	Chester	"	"	"	14	76	
Buswell, Noah *	Sandown	"	"	"	14	76	
Balch, Caleb	Westmoreland	"	Hinds's	"	14	76	
Barrett, Jonathan *	Hinsdale	"	"	"	14	76	
Belding, Elisha *	"	Corporal	"	"	14	76	
Belding, Moses	Swanzey	Private	"	"	14	76	
Brittim, Job	Westmoreland	"	"	"	14	76	
Bailey, Andrew *	Hollis	Sergeant	Spaulding's	"	14	76	
Bailey, Job *	Lyndeborough	Private	"	"	14	76	
Barker, Phinehas	"	"	"	"	14	76	
Batchelder, Nathaniel *	"	"	"	"	14	76	
Bevins, Edward *	"	"	"	"	14	76	
Boffee, Thomas *	"	"	"	"	14	76	
Bradford, Joseph *	Amherst	Lieutenant	"	"	14	76	

NEW HAMPSHIRE MEN AT BUNKER HILL.

Name	Town	Rank	Company				
Brown, William *	Amherst	Private	Spaulding's	Reed's	14	87	M.
Breed, John	Nelson	"	Towne's	"	16	52	M.
Breeden, Samuel	Temple	Sergeant	"	"	16	52	M.
Browne, Peter *	"	Private	"	"	16	52	M.
Browne, Josiah *	New Ipswich	Lieutenant	"	"	16	52	M.
Bullard, Ebenezer	"	Private	"	"	14	213	A.
Barker, John	Fitzwilliam	"	Whitcomb's	"	14	92	
Bishop, Samuel	Marlborough	Sergeant	"	"	14	213	A. P.
Boynton, Amos *	Fitzwilliam	Private	"	"	14	92	
Braman, David	Swanzey	"	"	"	14	92	
Brigham, Stephen *	Fitzwilliam	"	"	"	14	92	
Butler, Andrew *	"	"	"	"	14	95	
Balch, Hart	Wilton	"	Walker's	"	14	96	
Bayley, Benjamin *	Nashua	"	"	"	14	96	
Bayley, Eliphalet *	"	"	"	"	14	96	
Blanchard, Eleazer *	"	"	"	"	14	96	
Blanchard, Stephen	Wilton	"	"	"	14	97	
Blanchard, Stephen, Jr.	"	"	"	"	14	95	
Blodgett, Jacob *	"	"	"	"	14	96	
Brown, James *	Wilton	Lieutenant	"	"	14	96	
Brown, Isaac *	"	Private	"	"	14	95	
Brown, Daniel	"	"	"	"	14	96	
Butterfield, Simeon	Nashua	"	"	"	14	99	
Butterfield, William *	Rindge	"	Thomas's	"	14	101	
Beals, Benjamin *	Wilton	Fifer	Mann's	"	14	100	Killed.
Bales, William *	Mason	Private	"	"	14	101	Killed.
Barrett, Isaac *	Milford	"	"	"	14	101	
Bevins, Benjamin	Mason	"	"	"	14	101	
Blodgett, Jacob	"	Lieutenant	"	"	14	100	
Blood, Joseph *	Marlborough	Private	"	"	14	213	A.
Blood, Ebenezer, Jr *	"	Corporal	"	"	14	100	
Brewer, James *	"	Private	Crosby's	"	14	102	
Buxton, John *	Wilton	"	"	"	14	102	
Barrett, Nathaniel *	Amherst	"	"	"	14	102	
Bowtell, Joseph *	"	"	"	"	14		
Bowtell, Thomas	"	"	"	"	14		

Names.	Residence.	Rank.	Company.	Regiment.	Vol.	Page.	Remarks.
Bradford, William *	Amherst	Sergeant	Crosby's	Reed's	14	102	
Brown, Alexander *	"	Private	"	"	14	102	
Burnham, Joshua	"	"	"	"	14	102	
Burnham, Jonathan	"	"	"	"	14	102	
Barrett, John *	Hinsdale	Sergeant	Marcy's	"	14	104	
Burl, Samuel *	"	Private	"	"	14	104	
Ball, Ebenezer	Hollis	"	Dow's	Prescott's	14	76	M.
Blood, Nathan	"	Sergeant	"	"	14	76	M. Killed.
Blood, Ephraim *	"	Corporal	"	"	14	76	M. Wounded.
Blood, Francis *	"	Private	"	"	14	76	M. Wounded.
Boynton, Joshua	"	Sergeant	"	"	14	76	M.
Boynton, Elias *	"	Private	"	"	14	76	M. Killed.
Boynton, Jacob	"	"	"	"	14	76	M.
Brown, Abel *	"	"	"	"	14	76	M.
Brown, Edward	Exeter	"	Maxwell's	"	56	68	M.
Burt, Stephen	Stoddard	"	"	"	56	68	M.
Butler, Gideon	Hudson	"	"	"	56	68	M.
Bixby, Thomas	Litchfield	Sergeant	Moore's	"	56	65	M.
Badger, Nathaniel	Brookline	Private	Gilbert's	"	13	18	M.
Barron, Joshua	New Ipswich	Sergeant	Wyman's	"	56	66	M. Wounded and taken prisoner.
Bigelow, Benjamin	Nelson	Private	"	"	56	66	M.
Bizel, Robert	New Ipswich	"	Lawrence's	"	15	55	M.
Bacon, Retire	Peterborough	"	Corey's	"	56	64	M.
Brown, Michael	Exeter	"	Currier's	Frye's	56	1	M.
Banks, John	Alstead	"	Drury's	Ward's	14	72	M.
Brigham, Abner	Croydon	"	"	"	14	72	M.
Barroweliff, Samuel	"	"	Perkins's	Gridley's	14	47	M.
Bemain, George	Henniker	"	"	"	14	47	M.
Burley, Benjamin	"	"	"	"	14	47	M.
Chandler, Abiel	Concord	Adjutant	"	"	14	48	M.
Campbell, John	Windham	Private	Reid's	Stark's	14	74	M.
Campbell, Thomas	Londonderry	"	"	"	14	74	M.

NEW HAMPSHIRE MEN AT BUNKER HILL.

Name	Town	Rank	Company	Regiment		Age
Chase, Stephen	Londonderry	Private	Reid's	Stark's	14	74
Cherry, Samuel	"	"	"	"	14	214 A.
Christie, Peter	"	"	"	"	14	74
Clyde, William	New Boston	"	"	"	14	74
Collins, Solomon	Windham	"	"	"	14	75
Cressey, Richard	Londonderry	"	"	"	14	68
Cass, Theophilus *	Hopkinton	"	Dearborn's	"	14	68
Casey, John	Epsom	"	"	"	14	68
Clark, Jonathan	Northwood	Sergeant	"	"	14	68
Clifford, Israel	Deerfield	Private	"	"	14	68
Connor, Jeremiah	Gilmanton	"	"	"	14	70
Cram, Jonathan	Deerfield	"	D. Moore's	"	14	70
Cass, Daniel	Raymond	"	"	"	14	70
Cate, Samuel	Deerfield	"	"	"	14	61
Clifford, Dudley	Epping	"	Abbot's	"	14	60
Connor, Eliphalet	Pembroke	"	"	"	14	61
Call, Silas	Boscawen	"	"	"	14	60
Carr, Jonathan	Chester	Drummer	"	"	14	62 A.
Carter, Jacob	Concord	Private	"	"	14	215
Chadwick, Edmund	Boscawen	Lieutenant	"	"	14	61
Chandler, Abiel *	Concord	Private	"	"	14	61
Chandler, Peter	"	"	"	"	14	60
Clark, John	Boscawen	"	"	"	14	61
Colby, Ephraim	Concord	"	"	"	14	61
Connor, Joseph	Hopkinton	Corporal	"	"	14	61
Corser, Samuel	Boscawen	Private	"	"	14	61
Corser, William	"	"	Hutchins's	"	14	63
Corser, Eli	Chester	Corporal	"	"	14	63
Cromble, Hugh	Concord	Private	"	"	14	64
Currier, Jonathan	Warner	"	"	"	14	64
Carter, Hubbard	Concord	"	"	"	14	64
Chandler, Thomas	Hopkinton	"	"	"	14	64
Chase, Pratt *		"	"	"	14	
Clement, Nathaniel	Warner	"	"	"	14	
Clough, Joseph	New Boston	"	"	"	14	
Cochran, Elijah	Alexandria	"	"	"	14	64
Corliss, Eleinu						

Names.	Residence.	Rank.	Company.	Regiment.	Vol.	Page.	Remarks.
Cummings, Isaac	Canterbury	Private	Hutchins's	Stark's	14	65	
Clark, Jacob	Epping	Corporal	Kinsman's	"	14	66	
Clark, David	Brentwood	Private	"	"	14	66	
Clement, David	Bow	Sergeant	"	"	14	66	
Cotton, Benjamin	Gilmanton	Private	"	"	14	66	
Currier, Jonathan	Bow	"	Woodbury's	"	14	66	
Colburn, Merrill	Pelham	"	"	"	14	52	
Cole, Solomon *	Salem	"	"	"	14	53	Killed.
Collins, Thomas *	Windham	Lieutenant	"	"	14	51	
Corliss, Jonathan	Salem	Private	"	"	14	52	
Corliss, Emerson	"	"	"	"	14	53	
Currier, John	"	"	"	"	14	52	
Cutter, Richard *	Pelham	Lieutenant	Richards's	"	14	52	Wounded.
Carr, Jesse	Goffstown	Corporal	"	"	14	55	
Carr, James *	"	Private	"	"	14	55	
Carr, Thomas	"	"	"	"	14	56	
Carr, Samuel	"	"	J. Moore's	"	14	56	
Carr, Benjamin	Dunbarton	"	"	"	14	58	
Caldwell, Samuel	Bedford	"	"	"	14	58	
Callahan, John	"	"	"	"	14	59	
Campbell, Hugh *	"	"	"	"	14	58	
Cutting, Jonas	"	"	"	"	14	58	Wounded.
Cyphers, John * †		"	Baldwin's	"	14	211 215	A.
Carr, James	Hopkinton	"	"	"	14	51	
Chaffee, Clifford *	Walpole	"	"	"	14	217	A.
Chase, Jacob	Kingston	"	"	"	14	51	
Clement, Timothy	Hopkinton	Corporal	"	"	14	50	
Connor, Moses	"	Private	"	"	14	50	
Cooledge, Silas	Hillsborough	"	"	"	14	51	
Cressey, Daniel	Hopkinton	"	"	"	14	51	
Cunningham, Robert	"	"	Scott's	"	16	40	M. Killed.
Caldwell, Paul	Londonderry	"	"	"	16	40	M.
Caldwell, John	Windham	"	"	"			

NEW HAMPSHIRE MEN AT BUNKER HILL.   39

Name	Town	Rank	Company	Regiment			Notes
Caldwell, Samuel	Windham	Private	Scott's	Stark's	16	40	M.
Caldwell, James	"	Corporal	"	"	16	40	M.
Cochran, William	Stoddard	Lieutenant	"	"	16	40	M.
Church, Simeon	Marlow	Private	Stiles's	"	16	35	M.
Church, Thomas	Gilsum	"	"	"	16	37	M.
Church, Ildo	"	"	"	"	16	37	M.
Closson, Nathan	Walpole	Sergeant	"	"	16	35	M.
Cook, Ebenezer	Keene	Private	"	"	15	37	M.
Crossfield, Timothy	"	"	"	"	16	7 52	
Colburn, Nathan	Hollis	Corporal	Towne's	"	16	48	M.
Chaplin, Micah	Hampstead	Private	Hutchins's	Reed's	14	77, 83	
Clifford, John *	Candia	Sergeant	"	"	14	76, 81	
Copps, Ebenezer *	Hampstead	"	"	"	14	17, 81	
Couch, Benjamin *	"	"	"	"	14	76, 81	
Currier, David	Chester	Private	Hinds's	"	14	84	
Carlisle, Daniel *	Westmoreland	"	"	"	14	84	
Chamberlain, Ebenezer *	"	"	"	"	14	84	
Chamberlain, Henry	Westmoreland	Sergeant	"	"	14	84	
Cole, John *	Hinsdale	Private	"	"	14	86	
Cooper, Elijah	Chesterfield	S. M.	"	"	14	85	
Coughlan, Richard *	Francestown	Corporal	Spaulding's	"	14	87	[June 19, 1775.
Campbell, William *	Acworth	Private	"	"	14	85	Died of wounds
Campbell, James *	Lyndeborough	"	"	"	14	88	
Carleton, David *	"	"	"	"	14	88	
Carkin, Isaac *	"	"	"	"	14	85	
Chase, Joshua *	Hudson	"	"	"	14	88	
Colburn, Thomas	Litchfield	"	"	"	14	85	
Cowen, Isaac *	Lyndeborough	"	"	"	14	89	Deserted
Cram, Daniel	Hudson	Drummer	Towne's	"	14	87	
Currier, Samuel *	Lyndeborough	Private	"	"	16	52	M.
Carleton, Jesse	New Ipswich	Lieutenant	Whitcomb's	"	16	52	M.
Carleton, Nathaniel *	"	Private	"	"	16	92	M.
Cutter, Benjamin *	"	"	"	"	14	92	
Carter, Stephen *							
Chapman, Stephen							

† Undoubtedly John Piper, Wolfeborough.

Names.	Residence.	Rank.	Company.	Regiment.	Vol.	Page.	Remarks.
Chase, Ezekiel *	Fitzwilliam	Private	Whitcomb's	Reed's	14	92	
Cheney, Jesse *	"	"	"	"	14	92	
Clayes, Elijah *	"	Lieutenant	"	"	14	92	
Cobleigh, Eleazer	Chesterfield	Drummer	"	"	14	92	
Cummings, Nehemiah	Swanzey	Private	"	"	14	92	
Cummings, Enoch *	"	"	"	"	14	92	
Chandler, Moses		"	Walker's	"	14	96	
Chase, Stephen	Hudson	"	"	"	14	97	Died July 15, 1775.
Clogston, Paul *	Nashua	"	"	"	14	95	Wounded.
Coombs, Melad *	"	Corporal	"	"	14	95	Killed.
Cram, Asa *	Wilton	Private	"	"	14	96	
Carleton, George *	Rindge	"	Thomas's	"	14	99	
Cochran, James *	Amherst	"	"	"	14	99	
Campbell, Samuel *	Wilton	"	Mann's	"	14	101	
Carleton, Ebenezer *	Keene	Sergeant	"	"	14	101	
Carpenter, Ebenezer	Chesterfield	Private	"	"	14	100	
Colburn, Amos *	Marlborough	"	"	"	14	101	
Collins, Daniel *	Amherst	"	"	"	14	101	
Clark, Thomas	"	"	Crosby's	"	14	102	
Cochran, Robert	"	"	"	"	14	102	
Cole, John *	"	Captain	"	"	14	102	Killed.
Crosby, Josiah *	"	Private	"	"	14	102	
Crosby, Stephen	"	"	"	"	14	102	
Curtice, Jacob		"	"	"	14	102	
Calkins, John *	Charlestown	"	Marcy's	"	14	104	
Caswell, Gilbert *	"	"	"	"	14	106	A. P.
Chamberlain, Benjamin		Drummer	"	"	14	104	Died June 25, 1775.
Clark, Timothy *	Walpole	Private	"	"	14	104	
Clark, Hezekiah *	"	Corporal	"	"	14	104	
Conant, Jonathan *		"	"	"	14	104	
Cross, David *	Charlestown	"	"	"	14	104	
Cross, John *	"	Private	"	"	14	104	

NEW HAMPSHIRE MEN AT BUNKER HILL. 41

Name	Rank	Town		Regiment				Remarks
Campbell, John	Private	Hollis	Dow's	Prescott's	14	76	M.	
Chamberlain, Wilder*	"	"	"	"	14	76	M.	
Conant, Abel*	"	"	"	"	14	76	M.	
Cumings, John	Lieutenant	"	"	"	14	76	M.	
Cumings, Benjamin*	Private	"	"	"	14	76	M.	
Cumings, Peter	"	"	"	"	14	76	M.	Deserted Aug. 3
Cumings, Philip	"	"	"	"	14	68	M.	
Campbell, Thomas	"	Hudson	Maxwell's	"	56	68	M.	
Cumings, Reuben	"	Merrimack	Moore's	"	15	70	M.	Killed.
Clough, John	"	Plymouth	"	"	56	65	M.	
Colburn, Thomas	"	Nashua	"	"	56	65	M.	
Coombs, John	"	Merrimack	"	"	56	65	M.	
Conroy, Samuel	"	Hollis	"	"	56	62	M.	
Cowin, William	"	Merrimack	"	"	56	66	M.	Wounded.
Coneck, James	"	Brookline	Gilbert's	"	56	67	M.	A.
Campbell, John	"	Henniker	Wyman's	"	14	6	M.	
Cumings, Samuel	"	New Ipswich	Nutting's	"	56	7	M.	
Cobby, James	"	Hampton	Bancroft's	Bridges's	146	69	M.	
Campbell, Robert †	"	Newmarket	Ballard's	Frye's	56	7	M.	
Clough, Zacheus	"	Fremont	"	"	56	7	M.	
Colby, Theophilus	"	South Hampton	"	"	56	1	M.	
Cornell, Ebenezer	"	Rochester	"	"		269		
Colby, David	"	Newton	Currier's	Gridley's	14	74	M.	
Carney, Timothy	"	Portsmouth	Gridley's	"	14	74	M.	
Dickey, William	"	Londonderry	Reid's	Stark's	14	214	A. P.	
Duncan, James	"	"	"	"	14	68		
Dearborn, Henry*	Captain	Nottingham	Dearborn's	"	14	68		
Dearborn, Simeon	Private	"	"	"	14	72		
Dow, Jeremiah	"	Northwood	"	"	15	52		
Dow, Jonathan*	"	"	"	"	14	70		
Dorr, William	"	Dover	D. Moore's	"	14	60		
Dolloff, Noah*	"	Brentwood	"	"				
Davis, Samuel	Sergeant	Boscawen	Abbot's	"				

† In place of John Duch, prior to October 6.

Names.	Residence.	Rank.	Company.	Regiment.	Vol.	Page.	Remarks.
Davis, Nathan	Boscawen	Corporal	Abbot's	Stark's	14	60	
Davis, Isaac	"	Private	"	"	14	61	
Davis, Joseph	Plymouth	"	"	"	14	211	A.
Dimond, Ezekiel	Concord	"	"	"	14	61	
Danforth, Simeon	"	Corporal	Hutchins's	"	{17 14	3 63}	
Darling, William	Hopkinton	Private	"	"	14	64	
Davis, Wells	Warner	"	"	"	{17 14	3 64}	
Danforth, Joshua	Boscawen	Sergeant	Kinsman's	"	14	66	
Dearlorn, Samuel	Epping	Lieutenant	"	"	14	66	
Dearborn, Nathaniel	Chester	Private	"	"	14	66	
Dearborn, Sherburn	"	"	"	"	14	66	
Drake, Abraham, Jr.	Brentwood	"	"	"	14	66	
Dudley, Stephen, Jr.*	Gilmanton	"	"	"	14	66	
Duty, William	Salem	Corporal	Woolbury's	"	14	52	
Dustin, Obadiah	"	Private	"	"	14	53	
Dalton, Caleb*	"	"	Richards's	"	14	57	Killed.
Davis, Edmund	Dunbarton	"	J. Moore's	"	14	58	A. P...
Doblin, John	Bedford	"	"	"	14	214	
Darling, Moses	Hopkinton	"	Baldwin's	"	14	50	
Durant, Jonathan	Hillsborough	"	"	"	14	51	
Dassance, Jesse	Keene	"	Stiles's	"	16	37	M.
Day, Stephen	"	"	"	"	16	37	M. Wounded.
Dewey, Timothy	Gilsum	"	"	"	16	37	M.
Darrah, Robert	Litchfield	"	Towne's	"	16	48	M.
Davis, James	Hudson	"	"	"	16	48	M.
Dutton, Jonathan	Amherst	"	"	"	16	48	M.
Darby, David*	Westmoreland	"	Hinds's	Reed's	14	84	
Davis, Ezekiel	Chesterfield	Sergeant	"	"	14	84	
Davis, Jacob*	"	Private	"	"	14	85	
Davis, John*	"	"	"	"	14	85	Killed.
Dike, Benjamin*	Amherst	Corporal	Spaulding's	"	14	87	

NEW HAMPSHIRE MEN AT BUNKER HILL.

Name	Town	Rank	Company	Regiment				Notes
Dutton, Jacob *	Lyndeborough	Fifer	Spaulding's	Reed's	14	87		
Dutton, Ezra *	"	Private	"	"	14	88		M.
Davis, Elijah	New Ipswich	"	Towne's	"	16	52		M.
Dinsmore, Abraham	Temple	"	Whitcomb's	"	16	52		
Durant, Levi	Swanzey	"	Walker's	"	14	93		
Danforth, Jonathan *	Nashua	"	"	"	14	95		
Danforth, Abel *	"	"	"	"	14	96		
Darling, Timothy *	Wilton	Sergeant	Thomas's	"	14	96		
Davis, Benjamin *	Rindge	"	"	"	14	98		
Davis, Simeon *	"	Private	"	"	14	98		
Davis, David *	"	"	"	"	14	99		
Davis, Henry *	"	Corporal	"	"	14	99		
Demery, John	"	Private	"	"	14	98		
Demery, Ezekiel *	"	"	"	"	14	98		
Dole, Benjamin *	Jaffrey	"	"	"	14	99		
Dole, John	"	"	"	"	14	213		A. P.
Dutton, John	Mason	"	Mann's	"	14	101		
Davis, Benjamin	Amherst	"	Crosby's	"	14	102		
Dutton, Roger	"	"	"	"	14	102		
Debbil, Alexander *	Walpole	Sergeant	Marcy's	"	14	105		
Deming, Gamaliel *	"	Fifer	"	"	14	104		
Deming, Martin	"	Private	"	"	14	104		
Dodge, Zadoc *	"	"	"	"	14	104		
Downs, John *	"	"	"	"	14	104		
Dow, Reuben	Hollis	Captain	Dow's	Prescott's	14	76		Wounded.
Dow, Evan	"	Private	"	"	14	76		M.
Darrah, Arthur	Londonderry	"	Maxwell's	"	56	68		M.
Darrah, William	"	"	"	"	56	68		M. A.
Dean, Hiram	Jaffrey	"	Nutting's	"	56	65		M. A.
Dickey, Elias	Brookline	"	"	"	56	67		M.
Dunster, Henry	Mason	"	Farwell's	"	56	67		M.
Davidson, John	Nashua	"	Bancroft's	Bridges's	14	60		M.
Danforth, Jacob	Hollis	"	Stickney's	"	16	6		M.
Daniels, Joseph	Barrington	"	Ballard's	"	56	21		M.
Danielson, Charles	"	"	"	"	56	7		M.
Davison, Daniel	Hampton Falls	"	"	Frye's	56	7		M.
Dow, Jabez	Kensington	"	"	"	56	7		M. A.

Names.	Residence.	Rank.	Company.	Regiment.	Vol.	Page.	Remarks.
Dudley, Jeremiah, Jr.	Kingston	Private	Ballard's	Frye's	56	7	M.
Douglass, Alexander	Jaffrey	Fifer	Perkins's	Gridley's	14	45	M.
English, Thomas	Bedford	Private	Reid's	Stark's	14	73	
Emery, Noah	Pembroke	"	D. Moore's	"	14	70	
Evans, George	Allenstown	"	"	"	14	70	
Elliott, John	Boscawen	"	Abbot's	"	14	61	
Evans, Edward	Concord	"	"	"	14	61	
Eastman, Samuel	Henniker	"	Hutchins's	"	17	63	
					14	64	
Eastman, Ebenezer	Gilmanton	Lieutenant	Kinsman's	"	14	66	A. P.
Edson, Caleb	Croton	Fifer	"	"	14	214	
Emerson, Jonathan	Nashua	Private	Woodbury's	"	14	55	
Emerson, Eleazer	Goffstown	"	Richards's	"	14	56	
Emery, Joel	"	"	"	"	14	58	
Fagan, Luke	Bedford	"	J. Moore's	"	14	58	
Emerson, Charles	Manchester	"	"	"	14	58	
Emerson, George	"	Sergeant	Baldwin's	"	14	50	
Eastman, Moses	"	Private	"	"	14	51	
Eastman, Collins	Hopkinton	"	"	"	14	51	
Eastman, Enoch	"	"	"	"	14	51	Wounded.
Eastman, Thomas *	Peterborough	"	Scott's	"	16	40	
Emery, Richard	Keene	"	Stiles's	"	16	35	M.
Eddy, James	"	"	"	"	16	37	M.
Ellis, Benjamin	"	Corporal	"	"	16	37	M.
Ellis, Caleb	"	Private	"	"	16	37	M.
Emerson, Amos *	Chester	Lieutenant	Hutchins's	Reed's	14	81	
Emmons, John	Hampstead	Private	"	"	14	81	
Elmore, Elijah *		"	Hinds's	"	14	85	
Evans, Ira *		"	"	"	14	85	
Ellinwood, Joseph *	Lyndeborough	"	Spaulding's	"	14	88	M.
Elliot, David *	Mason	"	Towne's	"	16	52	M.
Elliot, John *	Peterborough	"	"	"	16	52	
Ellis, Joshua *	Keene	"	Whitcomb's	"	14	93	Wounded.

NEW HAMPSHIRE MEN AT BUNKER HILL.   45

Name	Town	Rank	Company			Notes
Estabrook, Abel	Fitzwilliam	Private	Reed's	14	93	
Emerson, Jonathan *	Nashua	"	"	14	97	
Emery, Thomas *	Rindge	"	"	14	98	
Earle, Caleb *	"	"	"	14	104	[ally June 19, 1775.
Eastman, Jonathan *	Walpole	Sergeant	"	14	105	M. Killed accident-
Eastman, Jonathan, Jr.	"	Private	"	14	76	M.
Eastman, Caleb	Groton †	"	Prescott's	56	74	M.
Elliot, William	Hollis	"	"	146	68	M.
Evans, John	Walpole	"	"	56	69	M.
Evans, William	Kensington	"	Frye's	14	1	
Elliot, Samuel	Newton	"	"	14	48	
Frink, Calvin	Swanzey	Asst. Surge'n	Stark's	14	74	A.
Fergason, John	Pelham	Private	Reid's	14	215	
Forrest, William	Canterbury	"	"	14	68	A.
Field, Andrew	Epsom	Corporal	Dearborn's	14	215	A.
French, Matthias *	Stratham	Private	"	14	71	
Pifield, Jonathan	Epping	"	D. Moore's	14	214	A. P.
Fogg, Jonathan	Raymond	"	"	14	71	
Folsome, Benjamin	Deerfield	"	"	14	71	
Frazer, William	Pembroke	Lieutenant	"	14	70	
Frye, Ebenezer	"	Private	Abbot's	14	62	
Fellows, Hezekiah	Boscawen	Sergeant	"	14	60	
Pifield, Abraham	Salisbury	Private	"	14	61	
Pifield, William	Concord	"	"	14	60	
Falanders, David	Boscawen	"	"	14	215	A. P.
Falanders, John	"	"	"	14	61	
Flood, Richard	Concord	"	"	14	62	
Foster, Joseph	Dunbarton	"	"	17	3	
Flanders, Micah	Concord	Drummer	Hutchins's	14	63	
Flanders, Thomas	Gilmanton	Private	Kinsman's	14	65	
Folsome, John *	Sanbornton	"	"	14	66	
Fox, Nathaniel *	Gilmanton	"	"	14	66	
Frohock, Thomas *	"	Fifer	Woodbury's	14	214	A.
Farrington, William	"	Private	"	14	52	
Farmer, James	Pelham	"	"	14	53	

† Name in 1775, Cockermouth.

Names.	Residence.	Rank.	Company.	Regiment.	Vol.	Page.	Remarks.
Foster, John	Pelham	Private	Woodbury's	Stark's	14	53	
Farmer, David	Manchester	"	Richards's	"	14	56	
Felix, Philip	Goffstown	"	"	"	14	55	
Flanders, Stephen	Bedford	"	"	"	14	55	
Fling, Patrick	Weare	"	J. Moore's	"	14	217	A.
Follensby, Moses	"	"	"	"	14	215	A.
Fellows, Moses	"	"	Baldwin's	"	14	215	A. P.
Fairfield, Jeremiah	Peterborough	"	Scott's	"	16	40	M. Killed.
French, William	Nelson	"	"	"	16	40	M.
Fletcher, Samuel	Marlow	"	Stiles's	"	16	57	M.
Fletcher, John	Walpole	Lieutenant	"	"	16	57	M.
Ford, James	Hudson	Private	Towne's	"	16	48	M.
French, Nehemiah	Hollis	"	"	"	16	48	M.
French, Joseph	"	"	"	"	16	48	M.
Frye, Isaac*	Wilton	Q. M.	Hutchins's	Reed's	14	76, 81	
Foster, Jeremiah*	Atkinson	Private	Hinds's	"	14	85	
Farnsworth, Silas*	Westmoreland	"	"	"	14	84	
Farwell, William*	Chesterfield	Sergeant	Spaulding's	"	14	87	
Fisk, Simeon	Mason	Private	Towne's	"	16	52	M.
Felt, Joseph	New Ipswich	"	"	"	16	52	M.
Fuller, Ezra	"	"	Whitcomb's	"	14	93	
Farr, Ephraim	Chesterfield	"	"	"	14	93	
Farr, Jonathan*	"	"	"	"	14	93	
Farr, Joshua*	"	"	"	"	14	213	A.
Fassett, Joseph*	Fitzwilliam	"	"	"	14	93	
Field, Waitstill*	Winchester	"	"	"	14	93	
Follet, Samuel*	Swanzey	"	Walker's	"	14	96	
Fosdick, Ebenezer	Nashua	"	Mann's	"	14	101	
Farr, Nathaniel	New Ipswich	Drummer	"	"	14	100	
Farnham, John	Wilton	Private	"	"	14	100	
Fish, John*	Mason	"	"	"	14	100	
Flagg, Isaac*	"	"	"	"	14	100	
Foster, Jonathan	"	"	"	"	14	100	

Name	Town	Rank	Captain	Regiment	No.	Remarks
Fuller, Silas	Mason	Corporal	Mann's	Reed's	14	100	
Fitch, Thaddeus *	Amherst	Private	Crosby's	"	14	102	
Flint, Amos	"	"	"	"	14	103	
Farwell, Isaac *	Charlestown	Lieutenant	Mary's	"	14	105	Killed
Farwell, Joseph *	"	Private	"	"	14	105	
Flood, Amos *	"	"	"	"	14	105	
Fowler, James					56	63	M. A. P.
Farmer, Minot *	Hollis	Sergeant	Dow's	Prescott's	14	76	M.
Farnsworth, David *	"	Drummer	"	"	56	7	M.
Felker, Josiah	Barrington	Private	Ballard's	Frye's	146	69	M. A.
Flanders, Jacob	South Hampton	S. Major	"	"	14	49	
Gray, James	Epsom	Private	Reid's	Stark's	14	214	A.
George, David	Londonderry	"	"	"	14	74	
Gilmore, James *	Windham	"	"	"	14	74	
Gregg, David	Chichester	"	Dearborn's	"	14	68	Wounded
Garland, James *	Gilmanton	Corporal	"	"	14	68	
Gilman, Jonathan	Lee	Private	"	"	14	68	
Glidden, Gideon	Deerfield	"	"	"	14	71	
Gilman, Ezekiel *	Raymond	"	D. Moore's	"	14	71	
Gordon, Josiah *	Brentwood	"	"	"	14	71	
Gordon, Timothy					17	3	
Glinds, Nathaniel	Canterbury	"	Hutchins's	"	14	65	
Gordon, John	New Boston	"	"	"	17	3	
Grace, Joseph	Concord	"	"	"	17	64	
Gilman, Moses *	Epping	"	Kinsman's	"	17	3	
Gordon, William	"	"	"	"	14	63	A.
Gordon, Joseph	"	"	"	"	14	214	
Gage, Jonathan	Pelham	Corporal	Woodbury's	"	14	65	
Gage, David	"	Private	"	"	14	67	
Gage, Abner	"	"	"	"	14	52	
Gage, Andrew	Salem	"	"	"	14	53	
Goodhue, Phinehas	Pelham	"	"	"	14	53	Wounded
George, Austin	Goffstown	"	Richards's	"	14	55	
Gibbs, James			"	"	14	55	

Names.	Residence.	Rank.	Company.	Regiment.	Vol.	Page.	Remarks.
Gage, Joshua	Dunbarton	Private	J. Moore's	Stark's	14	58	
George, Benjamin	Manchester	"	"	"	14	58	
Glidden, James	Dunbarton	"	"	"	14	58	
Glover, Henry *	New Boston	Drummer	"	"	14	58	
Goffe, John	Manchester	Private	"	"	14	58	
Gregg, John	New Boston	"	"	"	14	58	
Gates, Isaac *	Henniker	"	Baldwin's	"	14	50	
Gibson, James	Bradford	"	"	"	14	51	
Gilchrist, Richard	Peterborough	"	Scott's	"	16	40	M. Wounded.
Graham, John	"	"	"	"	16	40	M. Wounded.
Graham, William	"	"	"	"	16	40	M.
Gregg, Jacob	"	"	"	"	16	40	M.
Green, Thomas	Swanzey	"	Stiles's	"	16	40	M.
Gray, Hugh	Keene	"	"	"	16	37	M.
Gray, William	"	"	"	"	16	37	M.
Gray, Joseph	"	"	"	"	16	37	M.
Griggs, John	"	"	"	"	16	37	M.
Griswold, Isaac	Gilsum	Lieutenant	"	"	16	37	M.
Gage, Job	Salem	Private	Towne's	"	16	48	M.
Gould, Stephen	Amherst	"	"	"	16	48	M.
Greeley, Benjamin	Hudson	"	"	"	13	135	M.
Grimes, William	Londonderry	"	"	"	16	48	M.
Gilman, Israel *	Newmarket	Lieut. Col.	Hutchins's	Reed's	14	37, 80	
Goss, James *	Hampstead	Sergeant	"	"	14	76, 81	
Griffin, John *	Sandown	Drummer	"	"	14	77, 81	
Griffin, Theophilus	"	Private	"	"	14	77, 81	
Gross, William *	Chester	"	Hinds's	"	14	76, 81	
Goodenow, Nahum *	Westmoreland	Drummer	Spaulding's	"	14	84	
Glover, Robert *	Hudson	Private	"	"	14	87	
Glover, David *	Amherst	"	"	"	14	88	
Goodman, Richard	"	"	"	"	14	87	
Gill, Silas *	New Ipswich	"	Towne's	"	16	52	M.

NEW HAMPSHIRE MEN AT BUNKER HILL.

Name	Town	Rank	Company	Regiment			Notes
Griffin, Samuel	Temple	Private	Towne's	Reed's	16	52	M.
Gale, Asa *	Chesterfield	"	Whitcomb's	"	14	93	
Griffin, Abraham	Keene	"	"	"	14	95	
Gibson, Archibald *	Nashua	"	Walker's	"	14	96	Wounded.
Gibson, James	"	"	"	"	14	96	Wounded.
Gray, Jonathan *	Wilton	"	"	"	14	97	
Greeley, Joseph *	Hudson	"	"	"	14	99	
Gregg, Hugh *	Sharon	"	Thomas's	"	14	100	
Griffin, Dudley *	Jaffrey	"	"	"	14	100	
Gibson, John *	Mason	"	Mann's	"	14	101	
Goodenow, Adino	Marlborough	"	"	"	14	103	
Giles, Thomas	Amherst	"	Crosby's	"	14	103	
Gilmore, James *	"	"	"	"	14	103	
Goss, Peter	"	Corporal	"	"	14	103	
Greeley, Jonathan	Wilton	Private	"	"	14	103	
Greeley, Nathaniel	"	"	"	"	14	105	
Greeley, John	Unity	"	Marcy's	"	14	105	
Gilman, Stephen *	Marlow	"	"	"	14	105	
Gustin, Elisha *	Hollis	Lieutenant	Dow's	Prescott's	14	76	M.
Goss, John	Londonderry	Private	Corey's	"	56	64	M.
Giles, Richard	"	Sergeant	"	"	56	61	M.
Grimes, Moses	"	Private	"	"	14	6	M.
Gage, Samuel	Pelham	"	Bancroft's	Bridges's	14	60	M.
Gould, Gardner	Kingston	"	Coburn's	"	14	69	M.
Gilman, Daniel	"	"	Ballard's	Frye's	146	69	M.
Gordon, Caleb	Barrington	"	"	"	146	7	M.
Gould, William †	Fremont	"	"	"	56	7	M.
Grey, Moses	Hollis	Captain	Gridley's	Gridley's	56	269	M.
Gridley, Samuel	Londonderry	Private	Reid's	Stark's	14	74	
Head, John	"	"	"	"	14	74	
Holmes, Jonathan	"	"	"	"	14	215	A. P.
Holmes, Thomas	Windham	"	"	"	14	74	
Hopkins, John	"	"	"	"	14	74	
Hopkins, Allen	"	"	"	"	14	74	
Houston, Samuel	Londonderry	"	"	"	14	74	

† In place of Josiah Brown—Prior to October 6.

Names.	Residence.	Rank.	Company.	Regiment.	Vol.	Page.	Remarks.
Harvey, John *	Northwood	Private	Dearborn's	Stark's	14	69	
Hilton, John P.	Nottingham	"	"	"	14	216	A.
Hutchinson, Elisha	Gilmanton	"	"	"	14	69	
Hutchinson, Dudley	"	"	"	"	14	69	
Harper, William	Brentwood	"	D. Moore's	"	14	71	
Hoit, Thomas *	Alexandria	"	"	"	14	71	A.
Holland, Robert	Newmarket	"	"	"	14	215	
Holman, Jeremiah	Raymond	Corporal	"	"	14	70	
Holt, Nathan *	Pembroke	Private	"	"	14	71	Wounded.
Hall, Moses	Concord	"	Abbot's	"	14	61	
Hall, Stephen	"	"	"	"	14	61	
Harvey, Barnet	"	"	"	"	14	214	A.
Heath, Amos	Haverhill	Corporal	"	"	14	60	
Huntoon, Jonathan	Salisbury	Private	Hutchins's	"	14	44	
Holden, John	Canterbury	Captain	"	"	14	63	
Hutchins, Gordon	Concord	Fifer	"	"	14	63	
Hutchins, Levi	"	Sergeant	Woodbury's	"	14	52	
Hall, Benjamin	Salem	Private	"	"	14	53	
Hall, David	"	"	"	"	14	52	
Hall, James	"	Lieutenant	"	"	14	52	
Hardy, Thomas	Pelham	Private	"	"	14	53	
Hardy, Cyrus	"	"	"	"	14	53	
Hardy, James *	"	"	"	"	14	53	
Hardy, Jesse	"	"	"	"	14	53	
Harris, Joseph	Salem	Sergeant	"	"	14	52	
Hazleton, Jonas	"	Private	"	"	14	55	
Heath, Joshua	Goffstown	Sergeant	Richards's	"	14	55	
Hadley, Jacob	"	Private	"	"	14	55	
Hastings, Jonas	"	"	"	"	14		
Hutchinson, Timothy *	Manchester	"	J. Moore's	"	14	58	
Hart, Arthur	"	"	"	"	14	59	
Harvey, Lemuel	New Boston	"	"	"	14	58	
Hogg, James							

NEW HAMPSHIRE MEN AT BUNKER HILL.

Name	Town	Rank	Company	Regiment			Notes
Hogg, George	Bedford	Private	J. Moore's	Stark's	14	59	
Houston, James	"	"	"	"	14	59	
Hutchins, Nathaniel *	Hopkinton	Lieutenant		"	14	214	A. P.
					14	217	
Hutchinson, Solomon	Merrimack	Private	"	"	14	59	Wounded.
Hunter, John *	New Boston	"	"	"	14	59	
Huse, Thomas	Dunbarton	"	"	"	14	58	
Hadley, Ephraim	Weare	"	Baldwin's	"	14	51	
Hale, John *	Hopkinton	Lieutenant	"	"	14	50	
Heath, Robert	Sutton	Private	"	"	14	215	A. P.
Hildreth, Samuel *	Hopkinton	"	"	"	14	51	
Hills, Thomas *	"	Lieutenant	"	"	14	51	
Holt, Stephen *	"	Private	"	"	14	50	
Howe, Peter	Peterborough	"	Scott's	"	14	51	
Halfpenny, John	Temple	"	"	"	16	40	M.
Hillsgrove, John	Peterborough	Sergeant	"	"	16	40	M.
Hockley, James	Marlborough	Private	"	"	16	40	M.
Howe, Jonas	Keene	"	Stiles's	"	16	40	M.
Hall, Benjamin	"	"	"	"	16	37	M.
Hall, Hannaniah	"	"	"	"	16	37	M.
Harris, David	Surry	"	"	"	16	37	M.
Hayward, Nathan	Marlow	"	"	"	16	37	M.
Hayward, David	"	"	"	"	16	37	M.
Hayward, Joseph	Gilsum	"	"	"	16	37	M.
Holdridge, Jehial	Walpole	Lieutenant	"	"	16	37	M.
Holmes, Lemuel	Acworth	Drummer	"	"	16	37	M.
Hubbard, David	Marlow	Private	"	"	16	37	M.
Huntley, Nathan	Amherst	Major	Towne's	"	16	48	M.
How, Samuel	Rindge	Private	"	Reed's	14	80	
Hale, Nathan	Hampstead	"	Hutchins's	"	14	82	
Hale, Roberts	"	"	"	"	14	82	
Hall, Samuel	Sandown	"	"	"	14	82	
Hazeltine, Jeremiah	Hampstead	"	"	"	14	82	
Harriman, William	Raymond	"	"	"	14	82	
Henley, Samuel *	Sandown	"	"	"	14	83	
Heath, Zebediah	Hampstead	"	"	"	14	82	
Heath, Reuben	"	"	"	"	14	82	

Names.	Residence.	Rank.	Company.	Regiment.	Vol.	Page.	Remarks.
Heath, Richard	Hampstead	Private	Hutchins's	Reed's	14	82	
Heath, Samuel *	"	"	"	"	14	82	
Hildreth, Levi *	"	"	"	"	14	82	
Hills, Parker *	Candia	"	"	"	14	81	Killed.
Hills, John	"	Sergeant	"	"	14	82	
Hills, Reuben	"	Private	"	"	14	82	
Hutchins, Hezekiah	Hampstead	Captain	"	"	14	81	
Hutchins, Ephraim	"	Private	"	"	14	81	
Hutchins, John		"	"	"	14	85	
Hall, Jude	Kensington	Captain	Hinds's	"	14	74	
Hinds, Jacob *	Chesterfield	Private	"	"	14	85	
Hinds, Jacob, Jr.	"	"	"	"	14	85	
Howe, Samuel *	Westmoreland	"	"	"	14	85	
Hutchins, William	"	"	"	"	14	88	
Hardy, Thomas *	Hollis	"	Spaulding's	"	14	88	
Hardy, Phinehas, Jr *	"	"	"	"	14	88	
How, Ephraim *	"	"	"	"	14	88	
Hughes, Richard *	Amherst	"	"	"	14	87	
Hutchinson, James *	Lyndeborough	Sergeant	"	"	14	87	
Hutchinson, Samuel *	"	Corporal	"	"	14	87	
Hutchinson, Nehemiah	"	Private	"	"	14	88	
Hall, Daniel	New Ipswich	Lieutenant	Towne's	"	16	52	M.
Harkness, John *	"	Sergeant	"	"	16	52	M.
Hubbard, Elisha	"	Private	"	"	16	52	M.
Hutchins, Samuel *	Temple	Corporal	"	"	14	92	M.
Hammond, Joseph, Jr.	Swanzey	Private	Whitcomb's	"	14	93	
Harrington, Joshua *	Fitzwilliam	Sergeant	"	"	14	92	
Hastings, Josiah *	Chesterfield	"	"	"	14	92	
Heaton, William *	Swanzey	Private	"	"	14	93	
Hews, Benjamin	"	"	"	"	14	93	
Hills, Nathaniel	"	"	"	"	14	93	
Hutchins, Isaac	Winchester	"	"	"	14	93	
Hutchins, Asa	"	"	"	"	14	93	

NEW HAMPSHIRE MEN AT BUNKER HILL.

Harris, William *	Nashua	Drummer	Walker's	Reed's	14	95
Harris, William, Jr.*	"	Private	"	"	14	95
Harris, Jonathan	"	"	"	"	14	95
Harwood, James *	Wilton	Sergeant	"	"	14	97
Hawkins, William A.*	Nashua	Private	"	"	14	95
Hills, Simeon	"	"	"	"	14	96
Honey, Peter	Wilton	"	"	"	14	95
Howe, Israel *	Rindge	"	Thomas's	"	14	97
Hale, David *	Jaffrey	Lieutenant	"	"	14	99
Harper, John *	Rindge	Private	"	"	14	98
Henderson, Thomas *	"	"	"	"	14	99
Hobbs, Jacob	"	"	"	"	14	99
Hutchinson, Thomas	Wilton	"	Mann's	"	14	99
Haseltine, Nathaniel	Mason	"	"	"	14	101
Herrick, Joseph	New Ipswich	"	"	"	14	100
Hildreth, Simeon *	Mason	"	"	"	14	101
Holgman, Zacheus *	"	"	"	"	14	100
Holgman, Joseph, Jr.*	Wilton	"	"	"	14	100
Holt, Jeremiah, Jr.*	"	"	"	"	14	101
Holt, Simeon	"	"	"	"	14	101
Hutchinson, John	"	Fifer	Crosby's	"	14	101
Holt, Jabez *	Amherst	Private	"	"	14	102
Howe, Joel	"	"	"	"	14	103
Howe, Barzilla	"	"	"	"	14	103 [June 24, 1775.
Hutchinson, James	"	"	"	"	14	103 Died of wounds
Harper, Samuel *	Acworth	"	Marcy's	"	14	106 A.
Hastings, Sylvanus	Charlestown	"	"	"	14	105
Howard, Benjamin *	Sunapee	Corporal	"	"	14	104
Huntoon, Philip *	Unity	Sergeant	Dow's	Prescott's	14	76 M.
Hill, Samuel *	Hollis	Private	"	"	14	76 M. Killed.
Hobart, Isaac	"	"	"	"	14	76 M.
Hosley, Samuel	"	"	Moore's	"	14	65 M.
Haskell, Jason	Merrimack	"	"	"	56	65 M.
Hill, Ebenezer	Pelham	"	Coburn's	Bridges's	56	60 M.
Hoyte, John	Hampton Falls	"	Ballard's	Frye's	146	69 M.
Haskell, Job, Jr.	Fremont	"	"	"	146	69 M.A.
Hoit, Jonathan						

54 NEW HAMPSHIRE MANUAL.

Names.	Residence.	Rank.	Company.	Regiment.	Vol.	Page.	Remarks.
Huntoon, Samuel	Kingston	Private	Ballard's	Frye's	146	69	M. A.
Heath, Aaron	Alstead	"	Drury's	Ward's	14	72	M.
Hardy, Jacob	Salem	"	Perkins's	Gridley's	14	45	M.
Howard, John	"	"	"	"	14	47	M.
Hutchinson, Alexander	Londonderry	"	"	"	14	47	M.
Hills, Stephen	Amherst	"	Popkins's	"	56	273	M.
Ingalls, Israel	Sandown	"	Hutchins's	Reed's	14	82	
Ingalls, Simeon *	Rindge	Corporal	Thomas's	"	14	98	
Ingalls, Ebenezer	Jaffrey	Private	"	"	14	98	
Jenkins, Peter	Richmond	Sergeant	Capron's	Doolittle's	14	74	M.
Jackson, Joseph *	Londonderry	Private	Reid's	Stark's	14	68	
Judkins, Benjamin	Nottingham	Sergeant	Dearborn's	"	14	69	
Judkins, Jonathan	Deerfield	Private	"	"	14	71	
Johnson, Moses	Brentwood	"	D. Moore's	"	14	61	
Johnson, Isaac	Sutton	"	Abbot's	"	14	63	
Johnson, Peter	Concord	"	Hutchins's	"	14	64	Wounded.
Jenness, David	"	Sergeant	Woodbury's	"	14	52	A.
Johnson, William	Pelham	Private	"	"	14	216	
Johnson, Abraham *	Dunbarton	Corporal	J. Moore's	"	14	57	
Johnson, Calvin	Bedford	Private	"	"	14	59	
Jordan, John	New Boston	Corporal	"	"	14	57	
Jones, Moses	Hopkinton	Private	Baldwin's	"	14	51	
Johnson, Samuel	"	"	Hutchins's	Reed's	14	82	
Johnson, Oliver *	Westmoreland	"	Hinds's	"	14	85	
Johnson, John *	Lyndeborough	"	Spaulding's	"	14	88	
Johnson, Charles *	Chesterfield	"	Whitcomb's	"	14	93	
Jordun, Ebenezer	"	Corporal	"	"	14	92	
Johnson, Isaac *	Walpole	Private	Marcy's	Prescott's	14	105	
Jewett, Samuel *	Hollis	"	Dow's	"	14	76	M.
Jacobs, John	Merrimack	"	Moore's	"	56	65	M.
Jewell, Joseph	South Hampton	"	Ballard's	Frye's	146	69	M. A.
Jones, Josiah	Londonderry	"	Ames's	"	56	10	M.

NEW HAMPSHIRE MEN AT BUNKER HILL. 55

Name	Town	Rank	Company	Regiment			Notes
Kelley, Samuel	Pembroke	Private	D. Moore's	Stark's	14	71	
Kelsey, Moses*	Deerfield	"	"	"	14	71	A.
Kenniston, Winthrop*	Epping	"	"	"	14	214	Wounded.
Kimball, Abraham	Hopkinton	"	Hutchins's	"	14	64	
Kenniston, James	Epping	"	Kinsman's	"	14	67	
Kimball, Abraham*	Weare	"	"	"	14	216	A.
Kinsman, Aaron*	Bow	Captain	"	"	14	66	
Kinsman, Benjamin	Gilmanton	Private	"	"	14	67	
Knights, Francis*	Dunbarton	Sergeant	"	"	14	66	
Kimball, Oliver	Salem	Corporal	Woodbury's	"	14	52	
Kimball, Zilba	Pelham	Private	"	"	14	55	
Kimball, John	"	"	"	"	14	53	
Kincaid, John	Windham	"	"	"	14	53	
Kyle, Ephraim*	"	"	"	"	14	52	Wounded.
Kemp, William*	Goffstown	Sergeant	Richards's	"	14	55	
Kemp, Reuben*	"	Private	"	"	14	56	A.
Kerr, John	Belford	Corporal	J. Moore's	"	14	215	
Kimball, Reuben	Hopkinton	Sergeant	Baldwin's	"	14	50	A. P.
Kimball, Moses*	"	Private	"	"	14	216	
Kimball, Phinehas	"	"	"	"	14	51	
Kemp, William	Stoddard	"	Scott's	"	16	40	M.
Kelley, John	Walpole	"	Stiles's	"	16	37	M.
Kendall, Nathan	Amherst	Fifer	Towne's	"	16	48	M.
Keyes, Abner	Hollis	Corporal	"	"	16	48	M.
Knowlton, Asa	Pelham	Private	"	"	16	48	M.
Knowlton, Thomas	Hudson	"	"	"	16	48	M.
Kent, Peter	Hampstead	"	Hutchins's	Reed's	14	82	A.
Kimball, Moses	Candia	"	"	"	14	212	
Knowls, Amos*	Temple	Fifer	Towne's	"	16	76, 82	M. A.
Hilder, Wilder	Mason	Private	"	"	16	52	M.
King, Benjamin	Temple	"	"	"	16	52	M.
Kirkwood, Arthur	Fitzwilliam	"	Whitcomb's	"	14	95	M.
Kempton, Samuel	Wilton	"	"	"	14	93	
Kneeland, Joseph	Amherst	"	Crosby's	"	14	103	
Kenney, Archelaus*	Wilton	"	"	"	14	103	
Kittridge, Solomon	Wilton	Corporal	"	"	14	102	
Kingsbury, Eleazer W.							

Names.	Residence.	Rank.	Company.	Regiment.	Vol.	Page.	Remarks.
Kelcey, Seymore	Newport	Private	Marcy's	Reed's	14	104	
Keyes, Edward*	Acworth	"	"	"	14	104	
Kingsbury, Ebenezer*	Alstead	"	"	"	{14 15}	{105 752}	
Kemp, Thomas	Hollis	"	Dow's	Prescott's	14	76	M.
Kenney, Israel*	"	"	"	"	14	76	M.
Kinney, Samuel	New Ipswich	"	Wyman's	"	14	76	M.
Kemp, William	Stoddard	"	Crafts's	Gridley's	16	266	M.
Livingston, John	Londonderry	"	Reid's	Stark's	56	74	
Libbee, Josiah	Chichester	"	Dearborn's	"	14	69	
Libbee, Bennet	Epson	"	"	"	14	69	
Locke, Francis	"	"	"	"	14	69	
Locke, Moses	"	"	"	"	14	69	
Lawrence, Samuel	Brentwood	Drummer	D. Moore's	"	14	71	
Lovejoy, Obadiah	Pembroke	Private	"	"	14	70	
Lyford, Oliver S.*	Brentwood	"	"	"	14	71	
Loverin, Joseph	Kingston	"	Abbot's	"	14	215	A.
Lunt, Timothy	Chester	"	"	"	14	61	
Livermore, Daniel*	Concord	Lieutenant	Hutchins's	"	14	63	
Livingston, William	New Boston	Sergeant	"	"	14	63	
Livingston, Robert	"	Corporal	"	"	14	63	
Leavitt, Nehemiah	Brentwood	Private	Kinsman's	"	14	216	A.
Lamb, James	Goffstown	"	Richards's	"	14	56	
Little, Moses	"	Lieutenant	"	"	14	55	
Little, John	"	Private	"	"	14	56	
Lyons, James	Londonderry	Fifer	J. Moore's	"	14	55	
Lawler, David	Litchfield	Private	Baldwin's	"	14	215	A.
Leavitt, Brackett	Weare	"	"	"	14	216	A.
Lovejoy, Peter	Walpole	"	"	"	14	51	
Leonard, Solomon	Peterborough	"	Scott's	"	16	40	M.
Larrabee, Stephen	Keene	"	Stiles's	"	16	37	M.
Lewis, Eli	Marlow	"	"	"	16	37	M.
Lampson, Samuel	Amherst	"	Towne's	"	16	48	M.

NEW HAMPSHIRE MEN AT BUNKER HILL.

Name	Town	Rank	Company	Regiment			Notes
Lowell, Peter	Washington	Private	Towne's	Reed's	16	52	M.
Lane, John, Jr.*	Chester	Sergeant	Hutchins's	"	14	81	
Lane, John, 3d*	"	Private	"	"	14	82	
Leavitt, Nathaniel*	Hampstead	"	"	"	14	82	Wounded.
Leonard, Ephraim*	Westmoreland	"	Hinds's	"	14	85	
Lee, William*	Lyndeborough	Sergeant	Spaulding's	"	14	87	
Leeman, Samuel, Jr.	Hollis	Private	"	"	14	87	
Lowell, Samuel*	Washington	Drummer	"	"	14	88	
Lund, Jesse*	Lyndeborough	Private	"	"	14	88	
Lovejoy, Henry*	Wilton	"	Walker's	"	14	96	
Lovewell, Ichabod*	Nashua	"	"	"	14	95	
Lund, John	"	Sergeant	"	"	14	97	
Lake, Daniel*	Rindge	Drummer	Thomas's	"	14	98	
Lake, Enos	"	Private	"	"	14	98	
Learnard, Ezekiel*	"	Sergeant	"	"	14	98	
Leeland, Isaac	"	Private	"	"	14	98	Killed.
Lovejoy, Benjamin*	"	Corporal	"	"	14	99	
Lovejoy, Jonathan*	"	Private	"	"	14	99	
Lewis, Asa	Milford	"	Mann's	"	14	101	
Lowell, Timothy	Mason	"	"	"	14	100	M.
Lowell, Joseph, Jr.	"	"	"	"	14	100	
Lund, Stephen	New Ipswich	"	"	"	14	101	
Leavitt, Joseph	Amherst	"	Crosby's	"	14	103	
Leavitt, Andrew*	"	"	"	"	7	546	
Lawrence, Martin	Nelson	"	Nutting's	Prescott's	15	744	
Lund, Samuel	Nashua	"	Bancroft's	Bridge's	14	6	M.
Lankister, Samuel	South Hampton	"	Ballard's	Frye's	56	7	M.
Locke, Moses	Deerfield	"	"	"	56	7	M.
Leeland, Eleazer	Croydon	"	Drury's	Ward's	14	72	M.
Lampson, Jeremiah	Amherst	"	Popkins's	Gridley's	56	275	M.
McClary, Andrew	Epsom	Major		Stark's	14	48	Killed.
Mack, Joseph	Londonderry	Private	Reid's	"	14	73	
Mack, Archibald	"	"	"	"	14	73	
Mack, Robert	"	"	"	"	14	73	
Mackey, John	"	"	"	"	14	73	
McClary, David	"	Corporal	"	"	14	73	
McClure, James	"	"	"	"	14	73	

Names.	Residence.	Rank.	Company.	Regiment.	Vol.	Page.	Remarks.
McIlvain, Ebenezer	Londonderry	Private	Reid's	Stark's	14	74	
McMurphy, George	"	Corporal	"	"	14	73	
McMurphy, Robert	"	Private	"	"	14	73	
Miltimore, William	"	Sergeant	"	"	14	73	
Moore, William	"	Private	"	"	14	73	
Montgomery, Martin *	"	"	"	"	14	73	Wounded.
Montgomery, Hugh	"	"	"	"	14	73	
Morrison, John	"	"	"	"	14	74	
Morrison, James	"	"	"	"	14	73	
Marsh, Zebulon	Nottingham	Lieutenant	Dearborn's	"	14	68	
McClary, Michael	Epsom	Private	"	"	14	69	Wounded.
McCrillis, William	Nottingham	Sergeant	"	"	14	68	Wounded.
McGaffey, Andrew *	Epsom	Private	"	"	14	68	
McGaffey, Neal *	"	Corporal	"	"	14	69	
Moody, Josiah *	Deerfield	Private	"	"	14	68	
Moody, Clement *	"	Lieutenant	"	"	14	68	
Morrill, Amos	Epsom	Private	"	"	14	69	
Morrill, Jacob *	Nottingham	"	"	"	14	68	
Morrison, Robert *	Gilmanton	"	"	"	14	69	
Mudgett, David *	Deerfield	"	"	"	14	71	
Marston, Theodore	Pembroke	Sergeant	D. Moore's	"	14	218	A. P.
Martin, Nathaniel	"	Private	"	"	14	70	
McConnell, Moses *	"	Corporal	"	"	14	214	
McCullom, John *		Captain	"	"	14	70	
Merrill, Moses *	Deerfield	Lieutenant	"	"	14	70	
Moore, Daniel *	Pembroke	Fifer	"	"	14	70	
Moore, John	Bow	Private	"	"	14	70	
Moore, James	Deerfield	"	"	"	14	71	
Moore, Isaac	"	"	"	"	14	71	
Morse, Caleb	Alexandria	"	"	"	14	71	
Morrill, William	Deerfield	"	"	"	14	71	
Moulton, Nathaniel *	"	"	"	"	14	71	

Martin, Moses	Runney	Private	Abbot's	Stark's	14	210	A.
McCoy, James	Allenstown	"	"	"	14	62	
McFarland, Moses	Chester	"	"	"	15	751	
Miller, James	"	"	"	"	14	61	
Mitchell, William *	"	"	"	"	14	61	
McCoy, Charles	Concord	"	"	"	14	61	Killed.
McCoy, Charles	Pembroke	"	Hutchins's	"	17	211	A.
McNeil, Daniel	New Boston	"	"	"	17	3	
McPherson, Paul	"	"	"	"	17	64	
Morgan, John	Dunbarton	"	"	"	17	3	
Manuel, John	Bow	"	Kinsman's	"	14	211	A. P.
Meloon, Josiah	Epping	"	"	"	14	65	Killed.
Moore, George	Haverhill	"	"	"	14	65	
Moulton, Moses	"	"	"	"	14	65	
Mudget, John	Gilmanton	Corporal	Woodbury's	"	14	66	
Marden, David, Jr		Private	"	"	14	53	
McNelle, John	Salem	"	"	"	14	53	
Morgan, Jonathan *	Wilton	"	Richards's	"	14	53	A.
Manahan, John	Bedford	"	"	"	14	215	
McCarty, Charles	Goffstown	"	"	"	14	56	
McLane, Obadiah *	Litchfield	"	J. Moore's	"	14	56	A. P.
Martin, Nathaniel	Manchester	"	"	"	14	211	
Martin, Timothy	Francestown	"	"	"	14	59	
Martin, Samuel	Bedford	"	"	"	14	59	
Matthews, Joseph	"	"	"	"	14	59	
Matthews, Hugh	"	"	"	"	14	59	
McClary, Thomas	Merrimack	"	"	"	14	214	A.
McKnight, David	Manchester	Lieutenant	"	"	14	59	
McLaughlin, Thomas	Bedford	Private	"	"	14	57	
McNeil, John C. *	Manchester	"	"	"	14	59	
McPherson, James	New Boston	"	"	"	14	59	

Names.	Residence.	Rank.	Company.	Regiment.	Vol.	Page.		Remarks.
McPherson, John	New Boston	Private	J. Moore's	Stark's	14	59		
McQuig, David	Litchfield	Sergeant	"	"	14	57		
Mills, John*	Dunbarton	Private	"	"	14	59		
Moore, John*	Manchester	Captain	"	"	14	57		
Moore, David	Belford	Private	"	"	14	59		
Moore, Goffe	Manchester	"	"	"	14	59	A.	
Murphy, Patrick*	Belford	"	"	"	14	216		
McNeil, John	Hillsborough	"	Baldwin's	"	14	50		
Matthews, John	Peterborough	"	Scott's	"	16	40	M.	Wounded.
McAllister, Randall	Peterborough	Sergeant	"	"	16	40	M.	Wounded.
McClurg, Robert	Society†	Private	"	"	16	40	M.	Wounded.
McClurg, George	Peterborough	"	"	"	16	40	M.	
McKean, James	Peterborough	"	"	"	16	40	M.	
McMillen, Archibald	New Boston	"	"	"	16	40	M.	
Mitchell, James	Peterborough	"	"	"	16	40	M.	
Mitchell, William	"	"	"	"	16	40	M.	
Mixter, Timothy	"	"	"	"	16	40	M.	[21, deserted. Reported Aug.
Moore, James	"	"	"	"	16	40	M.	
Morrison, John	"	"	"	"	16	40	M.	
Munroe, Josiah	"	Sergeant	"	"	16	40	M.	
Mack, Jeremiah	Marlow	Private	Stiles's	"	16	35	M.	
Metcalf, Ezra	Keene	Sergeant	"	"	16	35	M.	
Metcalf, Luke	"	Corporal	"	"	16	35	M.	
Morse, Thomas	"	Private	"	"	16	35	M.	
Margery, Jonathan	Deering	"	Towne's	"	16	48	M.	
Marshall, Benjamin	Hudson	"	"	"	16	48	M.	
Marshall, Benjamin, Jr	"	"	"	"	16	48	M.	
Marshall, John	Londonderry	"	"	"	16	48	M.	
Merrill, Benjamin	Amherst	"	"	"	16	48	M.	
March, John, Jr	Danville	Lieutenant	Hutchins's	Reed's	14	81		
Merrill, Simon*	Chester	Private	"	"	14	82		
Mills, Levi*	Hampstead	"	"	"	14	82		
Morrill, Samuel*	Candia	"	"	"	14	82		Wounded.

NEW HAMPSHIRE MEN AT BUNKER HILL.

Name	Town	Rank	Captain	Colonel			Notes
Morrison, John*	Candia	Private	Hutchins's	Reed's	14	82	
Morse, Samuel	Chester	"	"	"	14	82	
Morse, Josiah, Jr	"	"	"	"	14	82	
McGinnis, John	Hinsdale	"	Hinds's	"	14	85	
McMichael, John*		Fifer	"	"	14	84	
Middle, John	Lyndeborough	Private	Spaulding's	"	14	85	
McIntire, Timothy*	"	"	"	"	14	89	
McMasters, Samuel*	Hudson	Sergeant	Towne's	"	14	87	M.
Merrill, William*	Temple	Private	"	"	16	52	M.
Marshall, David	New Ipswich	"	"	"	16	52	M.
Melvin, David	Temple	"	"	"	16	52	M.
Miller, Farrar	Peterborough	"	"	"	16	52	M.
Mitchell, Samuel		"	"	"	16	52	
Morrison, Thomas	New Ipswich	Corporal	Whitcomb's	"	16	93	
Morse, Elijah	Chesterfield	Private	"	"	14	93	
Merrill, Hallowell*	"	"	"	"	14	93	[as deserted.
Merrill, John*	"	"	"	"	14	93	Reported Sept. 11,
Metcalf, Joseph	Swanzey	"	Walker's	"	14	96	
Millins, Charles	Hudson	"	Thomas's	"	14	98	
Marsh, David	Rindge	"	Mann's	"	14	100	
Marsh, Obadiah*	Mason	Captain		"	14	100	
Mann, Benjamin*	Amherst	Corporal	Crosby's	"	14	102	
Miles, William	"	Lieutenant	"	"	14	102	
Maxwell, Thomas*	Walpole	Sergeant	Marcy's	"	14	104	
Mills, John	"	Captain	"	"	14	105	
Marcy, John*	"	Private	"	"	14	105	Died June 17, 1775.
Marcy, Samuel*	Hollis	Corporal	Dow's	Prescott's	14	76	M.
Melvin, John	Brookline	"	Maxwell's	"	14	76	M.
McConnor, James*	Londonderry	Private	"	"	56	68	M.
McIntosh, James*	Deering	"	"	"	56	68	M.
Mack, Archibald	Londonderry	Sergeant	Moore's	"	56	65	M.
Martin, Jesse	Merrimack	Private	"	"	15	70	M. [Aug. 10, 1775.
McClary, David	"	Sergeant	"	"	56	65	M. [oner. Died
Mack, James	Brookline	Private	Gilbert's	"	56	62	M. Wounded, pris-
McClure, William							
McCormack, Robert							
McIntosh, Archibald							

† Now the towns of Antrim and Hancock.

NEW HAMPSHIRE MANUAL.

Names.	Residence.	Rank.	Company.	Regiment.	Vol.	Page.	Remarks.
McDonald, John	Londonderry	Private	Corey's	Prescott's	56	64	M. [Aug. 10, 1775.
McFarlin, Joseph	"	"	"	"	56	64	M. [oner. Died
McGrath, Daniel	Amherst	"	Parker's	"	56	64	M. Wounded, pris-
Minot, Joseph	Hollis	Corporal	Bancroft's	Bridge's	14	4	M. Killed.
McLaughlin, Thomas	Amherst	Private	"	"	14	6	M.
Mitchell, Francis	Londonderry	"	Ballard's	Frye's	146	69	M.
Magoon, Moses	Brentwood	"	Drury's	Ward's	14	72	M.
Martin, James	Walpole	"	Perkins's	Gridley's	14	22	M.
Matthews, Thomas	New Boston	"	"	"	14	47	M.
McGilvary, William	Merrimack	"	"	"	14	47	M.
Moore, James	"	Sergeant	Reid's	Stark's	14	73	M.
Nesmith, John	Londonderry	Private	"	"	14	65	M.
Nesmith, James	"	"	"	"	14	68	M.
Nesmith, James, 2d	"	"	Dearborn's	"	14	69	M.
Nealey, John *	Nottingham	"	"	"	14	214	A. P.
Nealey, Andrew *	Deerfield	"	"	"	14	71	M.
Norris, Jonathan	Allenstown	"	D. Moore's	"	14	71	M.
Norris, Benjamin *	Pembroke	"	"	"	14	216	A.
Noyes, Moses	Bow	"	Kinsman's	"	14	56	M.
Nealey, Benjamin	Meredith	"	Richards's	"	14	39	M.
Newell, Andrew *	Goffstown	"	J. Moore's	"	14	37	M. Killed.
Newman, William	Bedford	Sergeant	Stiles's	"	16	37	M.
Nims, Asahel	Keene	Private		Reed's	14	88	M. Wounded.
Norton, Simon *	Chester	"	Hutchins's	"	14	93	M.
Newell, Pearson *	Marlborough	"	Whitcomb's	"	14	105	M.
Nott, Jesse *	Walpole	"	Marcy's	"	14	76	M. Killed.
Nevins, William, Jr *	Hollis	Sergeant	Dow's	Prescott's	11	76	M.
Nevins, Phinehas	"	Private	Ballard's	Frye's	56	7	A.
Nichols, James	Brentwood	"	Reid's	Stark's	14	215	
Orr, John	Londonderry	"	J. Moore's	"	14	57	
O'Neil, John *	Bedford	Sergeant					

NEW HAMPSHIRE MEN AT BUNKER HILL.

Name	Town	Rank	Company	Regiment			Notes
Orr, James	Bedford	Private	J. Moore's	Stark's	14	59	
Osmond, Henry	Londonderry	"	Scott's	"	16	40	... [24, as deserted.
Osgood, John *	Hudson	"	Spaulding's	Reed's	16	88	M. Reported Aug.
Oliver, Aaron	Temple	"	Towne's	"	56	52	M.
Otis, Paul	Barrington	Private	Ballard's	Frye's	14	7	M.
Parker, William	Londonderry	"	Reid's	Stark's	14	75	
Parkinson, Henry	"	"	"	"	14	75	
Patterson, John	"	"	"	"	14	78	
Patten, John	Bedford	Q. M. S.		"	14	216	
Page, David, Jr.	So. Hampton	Private	Dearborn's	"	14	69	A.
Page, David	Nottingham	"	"	"	14	69	
Petteugill, Abraham	Epsom	"	"	"	14	71	
Page, Joseph	Nottingham	"	"	"	14	71	
Page, Moses	Epping	"	"	"	14	214	
Perkins, Jonathan	"	"	D. Moore's	"	14	71	A. P.
Piper, Samuel	Pembroke	"	"	"	14	217	
Preston, William	Runney	"	Abbot's	"	14	64	A. P.
Palmer, James	Warner	"	Hutchins's	"	14	64	
Palmer, John	"	"	"	"	14	64	
Patterson, Samuel	New Boston	"	"	"	14	65	Wounded.
Patterson, Alexander *	"	Drummer	Kinsman's	"	14	67	
Perkins, Nathaniel	Canterbury	Private	"	"	14	66	
Perkins, William A	"	"	"	"	14	65	
Page, David	Epping	"	"	"	14	67	
Pease, Samuel	"	"	"	"	14	67	
Prescott, William	Dunbarton	"	Woodbury's	"	14	53	
Putney, Aaron	"	"	"	"	14	53	
Putney, James	Salem	"	"	"	14	53	
Parsons, Stephen	"	Corporal	J. Moore's	"	14	58	Killed.
Perry, William	Bedford	Private	Baldwin's	"	14	57	
Poor, Moses	Litchfield	"	"	"	14	51	
Patten, Samuel *	Hopkinton	"	"	"	14	51	
Patterson, William	Bradford	"	"	"	14	51	
Parsons, Noah	Hopkinton	"	"	"	14	51	
Presbury, Joseph	"	"	"	"	14	51	
Putney, Joseph							
Putney, John *							

NAMES.	Residence.	Rank.	Company.	Regiment.	Vol.	Page.	Remarks.
Putney, Asahel	Henniker	Private	Baldwin's	Stark's	14	51	
Page, Isaac	Londonderry	"	Scott's	"	16	40	M.
Proctor, Jeremiah	Stoddard	"	"	"	16	40	M.
Page, Jonathan	Weare	"	Towne's	"	16	48	M.
Parker, Samuel	Amherst	"	"	"	16	48	M.
Patterson, Adam	"	"	"	"	16	48	M.
Perry, Jacob	Londonderry	"	"	"	16	48	M.
Pollard, Timothy	Hudson	"	"	"	16	48	M.
Peabody, Stephen *	Amherst	Adjutant		Reed's	14	48	
Page, Moses	Atkinson	Private	Hutchins's	"	14	83	
Pettengill, Nathaniel *	Westmoreland	Corporal	Hinds's	"	14	84	
Powers, Josiah *	Hudson	Private	"	"	14	85	
Pemberton, James *	Nelson	"	Spaulding's	"	14	88	
Phillips, James *	Temple	"	"	"	14	88	
Patterson, Thomas *	New Ipswich	"	Towne's	"	16	52	M.
Pratt, Ebenezer *	"	"	"	"	16	52	M.
Prichard, Jeremiah *	"	"	"	"	16	52	M.
Parker, Amasa *	Swanzey	"	Whitcomb's	"	14	93	A.
Parkhurst, George	"	"	"	"	14	93	Reported Sept. 11 as having deserted.
Parkhurst, Samuel	"	"	"	"	14	93	Reported Sept. 11 as having deserted.
Parsons, Ebenezer *	Swanzey	"	"	"	14	93	A.
Potter, Joseph	Fitzwilliam	Sergeant	Walker's	"	14	93	
Putnam, Francis *	Wilton	Fifer	Thomas's	"	14	95	
Page, Lemuel *	Rindge	Private	"	"	14	98	
Page, Reuben *	"	"	"	"	14	98	
Parker, Samuel	"	"	"	"	14	98	
Parker, Benjamin *	"	"	"	"	14	98	
Pierce, Jacob *	Jaffrey	Sergeant	"	"	14	99	Wounded.
Porter, Nehemiah *	Rindge	Private	"	"	14	98	
Parker, William *	Wilton	"	Mann's	"	14	101	
Pettengill, Samuel	"	Lieutenant	"	"	14	100	

NEW HAMPSHIRE MEN AT BUNKER HILL.

Name	Town	Rank	Company	Regiment				Notes
Perry, Jonas*	Wilton	Private	Crosby's	Reed's	14	103		
Pettengill, Joshua	Amherst	"	"	"	14	103		
Powell, Thomas	"	Drummer	"	"	14	102		
Patten, James	"	Private	"	"	14	105		Died June 17, 1775.
Powers, Joseph*	Charlestown	"	Marcy's	"	14	105		
Prentiss, Simeon	"	"	"	"	14	105		
Prentiss, Thaddeus	Walpole	"	"	"	14	104		
Pulsifer, David	"	Corporal	"	"	14	105		
Pulsifer, John*		Private			14			
Patten, Nathaniel*	Brookline	"	Dow's	Prescott's	14	76	M.	Killed.
Pierce, Nehemiah*	Hollis	"	"	"	14	76	M.	
Platts, John	"	"	"	"	14	76	M.	Wounded.
Poor, Peter	"	Corporal	"	"	14	76	M.	
Powers, Samson	"	Private	"	"	14	76	M.	Wounded.
Powers, Francis*	"	"	"	"	14	76	M.	
Powers, Nahum*	Plymouth	"	"	"	14	76	M.	
Powers, Jonathan	Hollis	"	"	"	14	76	M.	
Pratt, Thomas*	"	"	"	"	14	76	M.	
Proctor, Ezekiel		"	Moore's	"	56	65	M.	
Perkins, Ebenezer	Peterborough	"	Corey's	"	56	64	M.	
Porter, David	Londonderry	"	Parker's	"	14	44	M.	
Parker, Jonathan	New Ipswich	"	Ballard's	Frye's	56	7	M.	
Page, Enoch	Nottingham	"	"	"	56	7	M.	
Parshley, George	Barrington	"	"	"	56	7	M.	
Parshley, Richard	"	"	"	"	56	7	M.	
Philbrook, Samuel	Greenland	"	"	"	56	7	M.	
Powell, Thomas†	Danville	"	Drury's	Ward's	14	72	M.	
Plumley, Joseph	Alstead	"	D. Moore's	Stark's	14	71	M.	
Quimby, James*	Brentwood	"	Hutchins's	"	{17, 14}	{3, 63}		
Quimby, John	Chester	Sergeant		"	14	77, 83	M.	
Quimby, Moses*	Hampstead	Private	Ballard's	Reed's	14	73		
Quimby, Samuel	Kingston	"	Reid's	Frye's	56	73		
Reid, George	Londonderry	Captain		Stark's	14	75		
Reid, Abraham	Windham	Lieutenant		"	14	75		
Roach, Thomas	Londonderry	Private		"	14	73		
Rowell, William	"	"		"	14	68		
Randall, James*	Nottingham	Fifer	Dearborn's	"	14	68		
Rowell, William	"	Private	"	"	14	69		

† In place of Benjamin Quimby prior to October 6.

NAMES.	Residence.	Rank.	Company.	Regiment.	Vol.	Page.	Remarks.
Runnels, John *	Deerfield	Private	Dearborn's	Stark's	14	69	
Rawlins, Joseph	Newmarket	"	D. Moore's	"	14	71	
Rawlins, John	Newmarket	"	"	"	14	71	
Roberts, Moses *	Brentwood	"	"	"	14	71	
Robinson, Richard	Raymond	"	"	"	14	71	Wounded.
Robinson, James *	Pembroke	"	"	"	14	72	
Rollins, Jeremy	Pembroke	"	"	"	14	71	A. P.
Runnels, Enos *		"	Abbot's	"	14	215	A. P.
Rawlins, Eliphalet	Runney	"	"	"	14	61	A. P.
Reed, Eliphas	Pembroke	"	"	"	14	215	A.
Robinson, John	Canterbury	"	"	"	14	215	
Rowen, John	Haverhill	"	"	"	14	61	
Ryan, John	Sutton	"	Hutchins's	"	14	64	
Roby, Jonathan	Sutton	"	Kinsman's	"	14	65	
Rogers, Samuel	Bow	"	"	"	14	65	
Rollins, Thomas		"	Woodbury's	"	14	53	
Rawlens, Eliphalet		"	"	"	14	217	A.
Roque, Bryan *	Salem	"	"	"	14	53	
Rowell, Lemuel *	"	"	"	"	14	55	
Rowell, Israel	"	Captain	Richards's	"	14	55	
Richards, Samuel	Goffstown	Private	"	"	14	56	
Richards, David	"	"	"	"	14	216	A.
Robinson, Joseph *		"	Scott's	"	16	40	M. Wounded.
Rowell, Samuel	Londonderry	"	"	"	16	40	M.
Raino, John	Andover	"	"	"	16	40	M.
Richey, James	Peterborough	"	"	"	16	40	M.
Richardson, Richard	Stoddard	"	"	"	16	40	M. Wounded.
Robbe, David	"	"	Stiles's	"	16	37	M.
Robinson, John	Londonderry	"	"	"	16	37	M.
Rice, Charles	Surry	"	"	"	16	48	M. Wounded.
Russell, Aquilla	Walpole	Corporal	Towne's	"	16	48	M. Wounded.
Read, William	Amherst	Private	"	"			
Robertson, Peter	"						

Name	Town	Rank	Company	Regiment			Wounded
Roby, James	Hollis	Corporal	Towne's	Stark's	16	48	
Reed, James	Fitzwilliam	Colonel		Reed's	14	80	M.
Randall, William	Chester	Private	Hutchins's	"	14	83	
Reed, Hinds *	Fitzwilliam	"	Hinds's	"	14	85	
Robbins, David *	Westmoreland	Private	"	"	14	85	
Robbins, Eleazer *	"	"	"	"	14	85	
Robbins, Samuel *	"	"	"	"	14	88	
Rolfe, Ephraim *	Hollis	Sergeant	Spaulding's	"	14	88	
Rowe, John	Lyndeborough	Private	Whitcomb's	"	14	92	
Reed, Sylvanus *	Fitzwilliam	"	"	"	14	95	
Robertson, William	Chesterfield	Corporal	Walker's	"	14	95	
Read, Abijah	Nashua	Lieutenant	"	"	14	95	
Robey, William	"	Private	"	"	14	95	
Robey, Philip A. *	"	"	"	"	14	98	
Russell, Jason	"	Lieutenant	Thomas's	"	14	99	
Raud, Ezekiel	Rindge	Private	"	"	14	98	
Richardson, Godfrey	"	Corporal	"	"	14	98	
Rogers, Timothy	Marlborough	Private	"	"	14	98	
Russell, Jeremiah	Rindge	Sergeant	Mann's	"	14	101	
Russell, Daniel	"	Private	"	"	14	100	
Russell, Joel	Westmoreland	Sergeant	"	"	14	101	
Randall, Benjamin	New Ipswich	Private	Crosby's	"	14	102	
Robbins, Jonathan	Marlborough	Sergeant	Marcy's	"	14	102	
Rogers, Levi	Amherst	Private	"	"	14	103	
Ramsey, David	Walpole	"	"	"	14	105	
Reid, Isaac *		"	Dow's	Prescott's	14	165	
Rice, Aaron		Lieutenant	Maxwell's	"	14	76	M.
Rokes, John *	Hollis	Private	Moore's	"	56	68	M.
Read, Jacob	Litchfield	"	Farwell's	"	56	65	M.
Russell, James	Merrimack	"	Ballard's	"	14	96	M.
Roby, Silas	Coös	"	"	"	56	—	M.
Russell, Peletiah	Hampton Falls	"	"	Frye's	146	—	M.
Rollins, John	Portsmouth	"	"	"	56	—	M.
Rowe, John	Barrington	"	"	"	56	—	M.
Rowell, Daniel	New Durham	"	"	"	14	47	M.
Runnels, Joseph	Londonderry	"	Perkins's	Gridley's			
Rogers, Samuel							

NAMES.	Residence.	Rank.	Company.	Regiment.	Vol.	Page.	Remarks.
Stark, John	Manchester	Colonel		Stark's	14	48	
Sargent, Valentine	Londonderry	Private	Reid's	"	14	215	A.
Senter, Asa	"	"	"	"	14	74	
Senter, Abel	"	"	"	"	14	75	
Senter, Samuel	"	"	"	"	14	75	
Smith, John	"	"	"	"	14	75	
Stinson, James	Dunbarton	"	"	"	14	75	
Stinson, Samuel	"	"	"	"	14	73	
Sanborn, Simon	Epsom	"	Dearborn's	"	14	69	
Severence, Peter *	Nottingham	"	"	"	14	69	
Sias, Samuel *	"	"	"	"	14	215	A. P.
Simpson, John	Deerfield	"	"	"	14	69	Wounded.
Sinclair, Noah	Loudon	Drummer	"	"	14	68	
Sargent, Aaron	Canterbury	Private	D. Moore's	"	14	214	A. P.
Sherburn, Job *	Epping	"	"	"	14	71	
Sinclair, Jacob *	"	"	"	"	14	71	
Stickney, Lemuel	Pembroke	"	"	"	14	71	
Stickney, Thomas	"	"	"	"	14	214	A.
Stinson, Robert	Salisbury	"	Abbot's	"	14	71	
Sanborn, Simeon	Concord	"	"	"	14	214	A.
Simonds, Timothy	Rumney	"	"	"	14	61	
Smart, Richard	Plymouth	"	"	"	14	61	Wounded.
Smith, Joseph	Newbury	"	"	"	14	215	A. P.
Stevens, Peter R	Concord	"	"	"	14	217	A.
Stone, Andrew	"	"	"	"	14	61	
Straw, William	"	"	"	"	14	61	
Straw, Thomas	Canterbury	Lieutenant	Hutchins's	"	14	65	Killed.
Shannon, George *	"	Private	"	"	14	63	
Soper, Joseph	New Boston	"	"	"	14	64	
Stone, John	Henniker	"	"	"	14	64	
Stone, James	Concord	"	"	"	14	63	
Straw, Samuel	Conway	Sergeant	Kinsman's	"	14	66	
Saltmarsh, Isaac							

Sanborn, John P.		Private	Kinsman's	Stark's	14	67
Shattuck, William	Boscawen	"	"	"	14	67
Sherburn, Samuel	"	"	"	"	14	67
Shirley, Alexander*	Chester	"	"	"	8	162
Shirley, John*	"	"	"	"	14	162
Sinclair, Edward	Gilmanton	"	"	"	14	67
Smith, Oliver	Meredith	"	"	"	14	67
Smith, Alexander	Brentwood	"	"	"	14	67
Smith, Nathaniel	Epping	"	"	"	14	67
Springer, Joseph	Haverhill	"	"	"	14	215
Spring, Seth	Conway	"	"	"	14	67	A.
Steele, William	"	"	"	"	14	67
Stevens, Jonathan	Dunbarton	"	"	"	14	67	Wounded.
Simpson, John*	Windham	"	"	"	14	53
Sargent, Elius	Goffstown	"	Woodbury's	"	14	56
Sinkler, Ebenezer	Weare	"	Richards's	"	14	56
Smith, Samuel	Goffstown	"	"	"	14	56
Stevens, Nathaniel	"	"	"	"	14	215	A. P.
Smith, Jonathan*	Dunbarton	"	J. Moore's	"	14	59
Stark, Archibald	Manchester	"	"	"	14	59
Stark, Caleb	"	"	"	"	14	51
Shattuck, Joseph	Hillsborough	"	Baldwin's	"	14	50
Simonds, Samuel	Hopkinton	"	"	"	14	51
Stanley, Benjamin	"	"	"	"	14	51
Stanley, John	"	"	"	"	14	51
Stickney, Duty	"	"	"	"	14	51
Straw, Richard	"	"	"	"	14	51
Scott, William	Peterborough	Captain	Scott's	"	16	40	M. [prisoner.
Scott, William	"	Lieutenant	"	"	16	40	M. Wounded, taken
Scott, William	"	Private	"	"	16	40	M.
Scott, Thomas	"	"	"	"	16	40	M.
Scott, John	"	Corporal	"	"	16	40	M.
Scott, James	Stoddard	Private	"	"	16	40	M.
Scott, David	"	"	"	"	16	40	M. Wounded.
Smith, Samuel	Bedford	"	"	"	16	40	M.
Stanford, Joseph	Nelson	"	"	"	16	40	M. [21, deserted.
Steward, Alexander	Peterborough	"	"	"	16	40	M. Reported Aug.

Names.	Residence.	Rank.	Company.	Regiment.	Vol.	Page.	Remarks.
Stinson, James	Peterborough	Private	Scott's	Stark's	16	40	
Swan, John	"	Sergeant	"	"	16	40	M.
Slade, John	Alstead	Private	Stiles's	"	16	37	M. A.
Stiles, Jeremiah	Keene	Captain	"	"	16	37	M.
Stone, Daniel	"	Private	"	"	16	37	M.
Seavey, John	Hudson	Private	Towne's	"	16	48	M.
Senter, Thomas	Londonderry	Sergeant	"	"	16	48	M.
Spaulding, Ebenezer	Washington	Private	"	"	16	48	M.
Stearns, John	Amherst	"	"	"	16	48	M.
Stevens, Caleb	Merrimack	"	"	"	16	48	M.
Sweat, Stockman	Hopkinton	"	"	"	16	48	M.
Scammel, Alexander	Durham	Brig. Maj.		Reed's	14	80	
Sanborn, Reuben	Chester	Private	Hutchins's	"	14	83	
Severence, Peter *	"	"	"	"	14	83	
Severence, William *	Londonderry	"	"	"	14	83	
Shannon, William	Chester	"	"	"	14	83	
Smith, Joseph	"	"	"	"	14	83	
Smith, Biley	Raymond	"	"	"	14	83	
Spillard, Joseph *	Chester	"	"	"	14	83	
Stevens, Peter	Sandown	"	"	"	14	83	
Stevens, Samuel	"	"	"	"	14	83	
Stevens, Moses	Hampstead	"	"	"	14	83	
Stevens, Asa	"	"	"	"	14	83	
Simonds, James *	Westmoreland	Sergeant	Hinds's	"	14	85	
Stoddard, David *	Chesterfield	Lieutenant	"	"	14	77	
Stone, Isaac	Westmoreland	Q. M. S.	"	"	14	77	
Stone, Ephraim *	"	Private	"	"	14	86	
Smith, Ephraim *	Hollis	Captain	Spaulding's	"	14	87	
Spaulding, Levi *	Lyndeborough	Private	"	"	14	88	
Starrett, William	Francestown	"	"	"	14	88	
Stearns, Benjamin *	Amherst	"	"	"	41	88	
Stearns, Isaac *	"	"	"	"	14	88	
Stiles, Samuel *	Lyndeborough	"	"	"	14	88	

Name	Town	Rank	Company	Regiment		
Scott, David	Peterborough	Private	Towne's	Reed's	16	52	M. Killed.
Scott, William *	New Ipswich	"	"	"	16	52	M. Wounded.
Severence, Abel	Temple	"	"	"	16	52	M.
Severence, Ebenezer	Washington	"	"	"	16	52	M.
Severence, Daniel *	Temple	"	"	"	16	52	M.
Smith, Benjamin	New Ipswich	"	"	"	16	52	M.
Soper, Samuel *	Nelson	"	"	"	16	52	M.
Stanhope, Isaac *	Temple	"	"	"	16	52	M.
Start, John	New Ipswich	"	"	"	16	52	M.
Stearns, Timothy	"	"	"	"	16	52	A.
Stevens, Jonathan *					14	221	M. [deserted.
Stevens, Ephraim					16	52	Reported, Sept. 11,
Stone, Josiah *	Temple	"	"	"	14	93	
Scott, Hezekiah	Swanzey	Fifer	Whitcomb's	"	14	92	
Smith, Joseph	Chesterfield	Private	"	"	14	93	
Stoddard, Eleazer	"	"	"	"	14	97	
Severence, Joshua	Hudson	"	Walker's	"	14	96	
Stevens, Theodore	Amherst	"	"	"	14	96	
Stevens, Henry	Wilton	"	"	"	14	95	
Stewart, Joel	Nashua	"	"	"	14	96	
Snow, John *	"	"	"	"	14	99	
Shaw, Caleb		"	Thomas's	"	14	100	
Scripture, Samuel *	Mason	"	Mann's	"	14	100	
Scripture, Samuel, Jr.	"	"	"	"	14	101	
Slack, Joseph	Swanzey	"	"	"	14	101	
Sloan, John *	Mason	"	"	"	14	102	
Stroud, John	Nelson	"	"	"	14	102	
Sawyer, Nourse *	Wilton	Sergeant	Crosby's	"	14	102	
Sawyer, Josiah *	Amherst	Private	"	"	14	103	
Simpson, James	"	"	"	"	14	103	
Small, Jonathan	"	"	"	"	14	103	
Stearns, Samuel *	Charlestown	Sergeant	Marcy's	"	14	105	
Spafford, Tyler		Private	"	"	14	105	
Stearns, William *	Charlestown	Sergeant	Dow's	"	14	104	
Stevens, William *	Charlestown	Private	"	"	14	76	M.
Spaulding, Jacob *	Hollis	"	"	Prescott's	14	76	M.
Stearns, Isaac *	"	"	"	"			

Names.	Residence.	Rank.	Company.	Regiment.	Vol.	Page.	Remarks.
Severence, Caleb	Londonderry	Private	Maxwell's	Prescott's	56	68	M.
Smith, John	"	"	"	"	56	68	M.
Sawtell, John	New Ipswich	"	Moore's	"	56	65	M.
Spaulding, William	Brookline	"	"	"	56	65	Wounded.
Spaulding, William, Jr	"	"	"	"	56	65	M.
Sheld, Daniel		"		"	15	55	M.
Sawtell, Jonathan	Rindge	"	Lawrence's	"	14	96	M.
Senter, Simeon	Londonderry	"	Farwell's	"	14	44	M.
Smith, Wadleigh †	Barrington	"	Parker's	Frye's	56	7	M.
Smith, Jethro	"	"	Ballard's	"	56	7	M.
Stowe, Jonah	Alstead	Corporal	Drury's	Ward's	56	227	M.
Sewell, Thomas	Lyndeborough	Private	Burbeck's	Gridley's	14	45	M.
Thompson, Joshua	Londonderry	Corporal	Reid's	Stark's	14	73	M.
Thompson, Samuel, Jr.	"	Private	"	"	14	75	A. P.
Thomas, Joseph	Deerfield	"	Dearborn's	"	14	214	A. P.
Thing, John *	Brentwood	"	D. Moore's	"	14	70	
Towle, William *	Raymond	Sergeant	"	"	14	70	
Towle, William, 2d *	"	Private	"	"	14	71	
Towle, Thomas *	Epping	"	"	"	14	71	
Tyler, Jeptha	Pembroke	"	"	"	14	72	
Taylor, David		Corporal	Abbot's	"	14	61	
Thompson, Samuel	Conway	Private	Kinsman's	"	14	66	
Taylor, Thomas	"	Sergeant	Richards's	"	14	56	
Taylor, Benjamin	Goffstown	Private	"	"	14	56	
Tiffany, Benjamin	Weare	Drummer	"	"	14	55	
Trussell, Reuben	Goffstown	Private	"	"	14	56	
Tuttle, Stephen	Litchfield	"	"	"	14	55	
Turner, John	Hillsborough	"	J. Moore's	"	14	59	
Taggart, James	"	"	Baldwin's	"	14	214	A.
Taggart, Robert	"	"	"	"	14	50	Wounded.
Taylor, William *	Hopkinton	"	"	"	14	215	A. P.
Trussell, Moses *	"	"	"	"	14	51	Wounded.
Taggart, John	Peterborough	"	Scott's	"	16	40	M.

NEW HAMPSHIRE MEN AT BUNKER HILL. 73

Name	Town	Rank	Company	Regiment			Remarks
Taggart, James	Peterborough	Private	Scott's	Stark's	16	40	M. Killed.
Taylor, Joseph	"	"	"	"	16	40	M.
Treadwell, Samuel	"	"	"	"	16	40	M.
Thatcher, Joseph	Keene	Corporal	Stiles's	"	16	37	M.
Tubbs, Frederick	Marlow	Captain	Towne's	"	16	37	M.
Towne, Archelaus	Amherst	Private	"	"	16	48	M.
Towne, Archelaus, Jr.	"	"	"	"	16	48	M.
Towne, Bartholomew	"	"	"	"	16	48	M.
Tuck, John*	Chester	Corporal	Hutchins's	Reed's	14	81	
Tarbell, Reuben*	Westmoreland	Private	Hinds's	"	14	85	
Taylor, Elijah*	"	"	"	"	14	85	
Thomas, Israel*	Hinsdale	"	Spaulding's	"	14	85	
Thompson, Andrew*	Lyndeborough	"	"	"	14	89	
Tuck, William*	Amherst	"	"	"	14	89	
Temple, John	Temple	Captain	Towne's	"	16	52	M.
Towne, Ezra	New Ipswich	Private	"	"	16	52	M.
Towne, Ezra, Jr	"	"	"	"	16	52	M.
Tufton, Thomas S.	"	"	"	"	16	52	M.
Toleman, Ebenezer	Fitzwilliam	"	Whitcomb's	"	14	213	A. P.
Toleman, William*	"	"	"	"	14	93	
Toleman, Benjamin	"	"	"	"	14	93	
Treadwell, Samuel	"	"	"	"	14	93	
Trowbridge, Luther	Fitzwilliam	Corporal	"	"	14	213	A.
Tucker, Moses*	Marlborough	Private	"	"	14	93	
Thomas, Philip	Rindge	Captain	Thomas's	"	14	98	
Thompson, John*	"	Private	"	"	14	99	Wounded.
Tarbell, Thomas*	Mason	"	Mann's	"	14	100	
Tarbell, Edmund	"	"	"	"	14	100	
Taylor, John*	Nelson	"	"	"	14	101	
Thomas, John*	New Ipswich	"	"	"	14	101	
Taylor, Jonathan	Amherst	"	Crosby's	"	14	103	
Trask, Rufus	"	"	"	"	14	103	
Taggart, James*	Charlestown	Lieutenant	Marcy's	"	14	104	
Taylor, Amos*	Walpole	Private	Dow's	Prescott's	14	76	M.
Taylor, Daniel	Hollis	"	"	"	14	76	M.

† In place of Daniel Buzzel, prior to October 6.

Names.	Residence.	Rank.	Company.	Regiment.	Vol.	Page.	Remarks.
Townsend, Ebenezer	Hollis	Private	Dow's	Prescott's	14	76	M.
Taylor, Silas	Stoddard	"	Corey's	"	56	64	M.
Twombly, Moses	Madbury	"	Ballard's	"	56	7	M.
Torrey, Joseph	Brentwood	"	Currier's	Frye's	15	746	
Tozer, John	Marlborough	"	Drury's	"	56	27	M.
Thompson, Benjamin	Westmoreland	"	Meacham's	Ward's	{15/56}	{61/170}	M.
Usher, Eleazer	Merrimack	"	Towne's	Woodbridge's	16	48	
Vance, John	Londonderry	"	Reid's	Stark's	14	75	
Varnum, John *	Candia	"	Hutchins's	"	14	76, 81	Wounded.
Veazey, Henry		"	Whitcomb's	Reed's	14	94	
Williams, Obadiah	Epsom	Surgeon		"	14	48	
Wyman, Isaac *	Keene	Lieut. Col.		Stark's	14	48	
Watts, Hugh	Londonderry	Private	Reid's	"	14	75	
Wilson, Thomas	Windham	"	"	"	14	75	
Wallace, John	Epsom	"	Dearborn's	"	14	69	
Wallace, John, Jr.	"	"	"	"	14	69	
Wallace, Weymouth *	"	"	"	"	14	69	Wounded.
Wells, Joshua *	Deerfield	"	"	"	14	69	
Welch, Thomas	Nottingham	"	"	"	14	69	
Whitten, Mark *	"	"	"	"	14	69	
Whitcher, Chase		"	"	"	14	68	
Wadleigh, John	Epping	"	D. Moore's	"	14	72	
Wells, Samuel	Hill	"	"	"	14	72	
Wiggin, Andrew	Newmarket	"	"	"	14	72	
Woods, Dennis		"	Abbot's	"	14	61	
Walker, William	Concord	Corporal	Hutchins's	"	14	63	
Webster, Joseph S.	Allenstown	Private	"	"	14	65	
Webster, Samuel	"	"	"	"	14	63	
Webster, Stephen		"	"	"	14	67	
Willey, William	Gilmanton	"	Woodbury's	"	14	216	A.
Watts, Jesse *		"	"	"	14	54	
Wheeler, Abner	Salem	Drummer	"	"	14	52	

NEW HAMPSHIRE MEN AT BUNKER HILL.

Name	Town	Rank	Company	Regiment			Remarks
Whiting, Nathan *	Pelham	Private	Woodbury's	Stark's	14	54	
Woodbury, Elisha *	Salem	Captain	"	"	14	52	
Woodbury, Elisha, Jr	"	Private	"	"	14	52	
Woodbury, Luke	"	Corporal	"	"	14	52	
Woodbury, Jonathan	"	Private	"	"	14	53	
Wells, Ezekiel	Goffstown	"	Richards's	"	14	56	
Wheeler, Plumer *	Dunbarton	"	"	"	14	56	
Wilson, Joshua	Goffstown	"	"	"	14	56	
Winn, James	Hudson	"	"	"	14	56	Wounded.
Wood, Edward	Goffstown	"	"	"	14	56	
Wood, Jonathan	"	"	"	"	14	57	
Wier, John	Merrimack	Sergeant	J. Moore's	"	14	59	A.
Wilkins, Andrew	Hillsborough	Corporal	Baldwin's	"	14	50	
White, Charles	Peterborough	Private	Scott's	"	16	40	M.
White, David	"	"	"	"	16	40	M.
Wilson, George	Stoddard	"	"	"	16	40	M.
Wilson, John	Peterborough	Sergeant	Stiles's	"	16	40	M.
Woodcock, Michael	Keene	Private	"	"	16	40	M.
White, Samuel	"	"	"	"	16	37	M.
Willis, Elisha	Gilsum	Lieutenant	Towne's	"	16	37	M.
Wilson, Daniel	Hollis	Sergeant	"	"	16	37	M.
Wright, Daniel	Merrimack	Private	"	"	16	48	M.
Wallingford, David	Amherst	Drummer	"	"	16	48	M.
Walker, Samuel	Merrimack	Sergeant	"	"	16	48	M.
Wheeler, Reuben	Hollis	Private	"	"	16	48	M.
Whidden, Samuel	Amherst	"	Hutchins's	Reed's	16	48	M.
Wilkins, Bray	Hampstead	"	"	"	14	83	
Wilkins, Jonathan		"	"	"	14	83	
Wadleigh, John *	Chester	Corporal	"	"	14	83	
Wadleigh, Thomas *	Sandown	Corporal	"	"	14	83	
Wadleigh, Jonathan	Atkinson	Private	Hutchins's	"	14	81	
Webster, Moses *	Chester	"	Hinds's	"	14	81	
Wells, Ebenezer *		"	"	"	14	83	Wounded.
Whittaker, Moses *		"	"	"	14	85	Deserted in Sept.
Wilson, Thomas *							
Wentworth, Lemuel *							
West, Edward							

NEW HAMPSHIRE MANUAL.

Names.	Residence.	Rank.	Company.	Regiment.	Vol.	Page.	Remarks.
White, John *	Chesterfield	Private	Hinds's	Reed's	14	85	
White, Samuel *	Westmoreland	Corporal	"	"	14	84	
Wilbore, Nathan	"	Private	"	"	14	85	
Witherell, David	"	"	"	"	14	85	
Winslow, Luther *	Hinsdale	"	"	"	14	85	
Wright, Jonathan	"	"	"	"	14	85	
Walker, John *	Hudson	Corporal	Spaulding's	"	14	87	Wounded.
Wellman, Jacob *	Lyndeborough	Private	"	"	14	89	
Wilkins, Elisha	"	"	"	"	14	89	
Wilkins, Robert R.*	Amherst	"	"	"	14	89	Wounded.
Walton, Josiah, Jr	New Ipswich	"	Towne's	"	14	52	M. Wounded.
Weston, Nathan	"	"	"	"	16	52	M.
White, Archibald *	Washington	"	"	"	16	52	M.
White, Daniel *	"	Sergeant	"	"	16	52	M.
Whittemore, Peletiah	New Ipswich	"	"	"	16	52	M.
Williams, Benjamin *	"	Corporal	"	"	16	52	M.
Wilson, Supply	Chesterfield	Private	Whitcomb's	"	14	94	
Walton, Elisha *	"	"	"	"	14	94	
Walton, Elijah	"	"	"	"	14	94	
Wheeler, Benjamin	Swanzey	Captain	"	"	14	92	
Whitcomb, Jonathan *	"	Private	"	"	14	94	
Whitcomb, Abijah *	Fitzwilliam	"	"	"	14	94	
Whitney, John *	"	"	"	"	14	94	
Whitney, John, 2d	"	"	"	"	14	94	
Wilson, Samuel	"	"	"	"	14	94	
Wood, Jonathan	Winchester	"	"	"	14	94	
Walker, William *	Nashua	Captain	Walker's	"	14	95	
Warner, Daniel	"	Sergeant	"	"	14	95	
Whitney, Phinehas *	Nashua	Corporal	"	"	14	95	
Whitney, Benjamin *	"	Private	"	"	14	95	
Winn, Nehemiah *	Hudson	"	"	"	14	97	

NEW HAMPSHIRE MEN AT BUNKER HILL. 77

Name	Town	Rank	Captain	Colonel			[11, 1775. Reported dead Sept.
Wood, Paul	Nashua	Fifer	Walker's	Reel's	14	95	
Wood, Oliver	"	Private	"	"	14	97	
Wright, Nehemiah	"	"	"	"	14	97	
Webster, Peter *	Rindge	"	"	"	14	99	
Wetherbee, Hezekiah	"	"	Thomas's	"	14	99	
Winn, Caleb *	"	"	"	"	14	99	
Wright, Joseph	Jaffrey	"	"	"	14	98	
Woolson, George *	New Ipswich	"	"	"	14	101	A.
Worsley, Robert *	Keene	"	Mann's	"	14	213	
Wright, Samuel *	Swanzey	"	"	"	14	101	
Wakefield, Ebenezer *	Amherst	"	Crosby's	"	14	103	
Wakefield, Joseph *	"	"	"	"	14	103	
Wallace, Joseph *	"	"	"	"	14	103	
Weston, Sutherick	"	Lieutenant	"	"	14	102	
Wilkins, Daniel, Jr.*	"	Corporal	"	"	14	102	
Wilkins, Eli	"	Private	"	"	14	102	
Wilkins, Jonathan *	"	"	"	"	14	103	
Williams, Samuel *	"	"	"	"	14	103	
Winchester, Lemuel *	"	Corporal	"	"	14	102	
Wright, Isaac	"	Private	"	"	14	102	
Warren, Cornelius *		"	Marcy's	"	14	105	
Watkins, Elias *		"	"	"	14	105	
Wheat, Thomas, Jr	Hollis	"	Dow's	Prescott's	14	76	M. Killed.
Wheeler, Lebbeus *	"	"	"	"	14	76	M. Wounded.
Wood, William	"	"	"	"	14	76	M.
Worcester, Noah, Jr.*	"	Fifer	"	"	14	76	M.
Wright, Uriah *	Merrimack	Private	"	"	14	76	M.
Walker, Zachens	Hollis	Lieutenant	Moore's	"	56	65	M.
Wright, Samuel	Londonderry	Private	"	"	56	65	M.
Wier, James	Hudson	"	Corey's	"	56	64	M.
Whittemore, Benjamin	Hampton Falls	"	Bancroft's	Bridges's	14	6	M.
Ward, Melcher	Nottingham	"	Ballard's	Frye's	56	7	M.
Welch, Matthias	"	"	"	"	56	7	M.
Welch, Benjamin	"	"	"	"	56	7	M.
Worker, Joseph	Portsmouth	"	"	"	146	69	M.
Wyman, John †	"	"	"	"	56	7	M.
Wardwell, Jeremiah	Pembroke	"	Ames's	"	56	10	M. A.

† In place of Benjamin Clough, prior to October 6.

NAMES.	Residence.	Rank.	Company.	Regiment.	Vol.	Page.	Remarks.
Wardwell, Ezekiel	Pembroke	Private	Ames's	Frye's	56	10	M.
Wadsworth, Ebenezer	Alstead	"	Drury's	Ward's	14	72	M.
Whitcomb, Simon	Jaffrey	"	Perkins's	Gridley's	14	47	M.
Whitehorn, Enoch	Somersworth	"	Gridley's	"	56	269	M.
Young, Jothan	Canterbury	"	Hutchins's	Stark's	{17 / 14}	{3 / 65}	
Young, Joseph	Gilsum	"	Stiles's	"	16	37	M.
Youngman, Ebenezer	Hollis	"	Moore's	Prescott's	56	65	M.
Young, Jonathan	Kingston	"	Ballard's	Frye's	146	69	M.
Young, David	"	"	"	"	56	7	Killed.

NEW HAMPSHIRE MEN AT BUNKER HILL. 79

MEN FROM CONNECTICUT, MASSACHUSETTS, AND VERMONT IN NEW HAMPSHIRE COMPANIES AT BUNKER HILL, JUNE 17, 1775.

Names.	Residence.	Rank.	Company.	Regiment.	Vol.	Page.	Remarks.
Parks, Joseph *	Salisbury	Private	Marcy's	Reed's	14	213	A. Conn.
Kanady, James	Colrain	"	Scott's	Stark's	16	40	M. Mass.
Marshall, James	Bridgewater	"	"	"	16	40	M. "
Read, Daniel	Medford	Drummer	"	"	16	40	M. "
Tucker, John	Newbury	Private	"	"	16	40	M. "
Busby, Robert	Medford	"	Stiles's	"	16	37	M. "
Richardson, Andrew	Tewksbury	"	Towne's	"	13	135	M. "
Swan, Caleb	Methuen	Corporal	"	"	13	135	M. "
Winman, James	Woburn	Private	"	"	13	135	M. "
Osgood, David	Medford	Chaplain	"	"	13	48	Mass.
Burton, Josiah *	Norwich	Corporal	Whitcomb's	Reed's	14	92	Vermont.
Chamberlain, Moses	Newbury	Private	Walker's	"	14	96	"
Chamberlain, Silas *	"	"	"	"	14	97	"
Lovewell, John *	"	Corporal	"	"	14	95	"
Lovewell, Nehemiah *	"	Private	"	"	14	97	"
Lovewell, Henry *	"	"	"	"	14	97	"
Taplin, Mansfield *	Pomfret	"	"	"	14	97	"
Clark, Thomas	Pomfret	"	Stiles's	Stark's	16	57	M. Vermont.
Hall, Samuel	Rockingham	"	"	"	16	37	M. "

NEW HAMPSHIRE SOLDIERS, NOT IN THE BATTLE OF BUNKER HILL, FROM OTHER REGIMENTS, IN THE ARNOLD EXPEDITION TO QUEBEC.

Names.	Residence.	Company.	Regiment.	Remarks.
Butterfield, Daniel	Conway	Baker's	Gerrish's	M.
Danforth, Elkanah	Tamworth	Clough's	Poor's	A. P.
Douglass, Thomas	Keene	Gould's	Sargent's	M.
George, Jonathan	Londonderry	Perry's	"	M.
Gilman, John M	Andover	Clough's		
Hews, Samuel	Lyne	Dearborn's	Poor's	A. P.
Hilton, Charles		"		A. P.
Mudget, Charles				A. P.
Mulergan, Edward	Londonderry	Gleason's	Nixon's	M.
Patch, David	Charlestown	Kellogg's	Ward's	M.
Robinson, John	Allenstown	Norris's	Poor's	
Rowe, John	Chester	Cogswell's	Gerrish's	M.
Stiles, Eli	Hollis	Worthley's	31st	M.
Tolley, Thomas	Dover	Titcomb's	Poor's	

REPORT OF SPECIAL COMMISSIONER.

To His Excellency Hiram A. Tuttle, Governor, and the Honorable Council:

January 24, 1889, the following order was submitted to the city council of Boston, and February 6 it was passed unanimously and approved by the mayor:

"*Ordered*, That a special committee of five members of the common council, with such as the board of aldermen may join, be appointed to arrange and prepare four bronze tablets, to bear the names of the American patriots killed or fatally injured at Bunker Hill, June 17, 1775; said tablets to embrace the requisite list of names now in the hands of the record commissioner, with such other names that belong in the list; said tablets to be completed in season for erection on the occasion of the coming celebration of the anniversary of the battle of Bunker Hill, June 17, 1889; said tablets to be placed in such position as the committee may determine in connection with the site of the battle."

The design of the committee, to place the four memorial tablets at or near the entrance of Monument Square, not being approved by the directors of the Bunker Hill Monument association, who control the same, they were placed on Winthrop square, Charlestown. The city of Boston published the proceedings at the celebration the following 17th of June, at the dedication of the memorial tablets, in an elegant volume, "A Memorial of the American Patriots who fell at the Battle of Bunker Hill, June 17, 1775, with an account of the Dedication of the Memorial Tablets on Winthrop Square, Charlestown, June 17, 1889," containing the oration delivered on the occasion by Hon. John R. Murphy, and also the orations of Daniel Webster, delivered June 17, 1825, at the laying of the corner-stone of the Bunker Hill monument, and on its completion, June 17, 1843, a copy of which can be found in the State library.

New Hampshire having an interest in common with Massachusetts to perpetuate in bronze the names of her dead patriots who gave up their lives at Bunker Hill, Governor Sawyer and council appointed the writer special commissioner to confer with the committee appointed by the city council of Boston, and furnish them with the names of New Hampshire men killed or mortally wounded, to be placed on the proposed memorial tablets. A printed list of names was furnished the Hon. William H. Whitmore, chairman of the board of record commissioners of Boston, who was preparing the list of names to be placed on the memorial tablets, and by him substantially adopted; what was most desired, however,—that one of the four proposed be made a distinctive New Hampshire tablet, on which to place all the names of the men from this state,—was not granted; the main objection to them as finally arranged was placing the names of the New Hampshire officers killed with those from Massachusetts, without designating their former residence. The printed list furnished Mr. Whitmore is herewith reprinted, with additions and corrections time has developed, and I most sincerely hope that the day is not far distant when a bronze tablet will be erected in the State Capitol park to the memory of the brave men from New Hampshire who perished at Bunker Hill.

To Mr. Whitmore the writer is under great obligation for courtesies extended and documents furnished him, and also to the Honorable Secretary of State of Massachusetts, and his assistants, Messrs. Strong and Tracy, for unlimited research of the papers on file in his office.

REPORT OF SPECIAL COMMISSIONER. 83

NEW HAMPSHIRE MEN KILLED OR MORTALLY WOUNDED AT BUNKER HILL, JUNE 17, 1775.

No.	NAME.	Rank.	Where from.	Regiment.	Company.	State Papers. Vol.	Page.	Swett's Notes. Page.
1	Adams, Isaac	Private	Rindge	Reed's	Thomas's	14	99	28
2	Baldwin, Isaac	Captain	Hillsborough	Stark's	Baldwin's	14	50	51
3	Blood, Joseph	Private	Mason	Reed's	Mann's	14	101	28
4	Blood, Ebenezer, Jr					14	101	28
5	Blood, Nathan *	Sergeant	Hollis	Prescott's	Dow's	15	743	
6	Boynton, Jacob *	Private	"	"	"	15	744	
7	Collins, Thomas	"	Windham	Stark's	Woodbury's	14	54	28
8	Caldwell, Paul	"	Londonderry	"	Scott's	15	740	
9	Carleton, David †	"	Lyndeborough	Reed's	Spaulding's	14	88	28
10	Carleton, George	"	Rindge	"	Thomas's	14	99	28
11	Cole, John	"	Amherst	"	Crosby's	14	102	28
12	Colbourne, Thomas	"	Nashua	Prescott's	Moore's	14	745	
13	Dalton, Caleb	"		Stark'y	Richards's	14	57	28
14	Davis, John ‡	"	Chesterfield	Reed's	Hinds's	14	85	28
15	French, William	"	Nelson	Stark's	Scott's	15	740	
16	Farwell, Joseph	"	Charlestown	"	Marcy's	14	105	28
17	Howe, Jonas	"	Marlborough	Reed's	Scott's	15	740	
18	Hills, Parker	"	Candia	Stark's	H. Hutchins's	14	82	28
19	Hutchinson, James ‖	"	Amherst	Reed's	Crosby's	14	103	28
20	Hobart, Isaac *	"	Hollis	Prescott's	Dow's	15	744	
21	Lovejoy, Jonathan		Rindge	Reed's	Thomas's	14	99	28
22	McClary, Andrew	Major	Epson	Stark's		14	48	30
23	Mitchell, William	Private	Concord	"	Abbott's	14	61	28
24	Manuel, John	"	Bow	"	Kinsman's	14	67	28
25	McIntosh, Archibald §	"	Brookline	Prescott's	Gilbert's	15	745	23
26	Nims, Asahel	Sergeant	Keene	Stark's	Stiles's	15	741	
27	Nevins, Phineas ¶	Private	Hollis	Prescotts	Dow's	14	744	26
28	Poor, Moses	"		Stark's	Woodbury's	14	53	28

*History Hollis, pp. 154, 203–205. † Wounded, died June 19. Swett's Notes, "killed." ‡ In roll printed "Daws"; Swett's Notes, "Dane." ‖ Wounded, died June 24; Swett's Notes, "killed." § Wounded, prisoner; d. August 10.
¶ Wounded, prisoner; in Swett's Notes printed, "Nevers, killed."

NEW HAMPSHIRE MEN KILLED OR MORTALLY WOUNDED AT BUNKER HILL, JUNE 17, 1775.

No.	NAME.	Rank.	Where from.	Regiment.	Company.	State Papers. Vol.	Page.	Swetts's Notes. Page.
29	Poor, Peter	Private	Hollis	Prescott's	Dow's	15	744	
30	Shannon, George	"	Canterbury	Stark's	G. Hutchins's	14	65	28
31	Scott, David	"	Peterborough	Reed's	E. Towne's	14	91	28
32	Taylor, Joseph	"	"	Stark's	Scott's	15	739	
33	Wheat, Thomas, Jr.	"	Hollis	Prescott's	Dow's	15	744	
34	Youngman, Ebenezer	"	"	Reed's	Moore's	15	745	
35	Clogstone, Paul *	"	Nashua	Reed's	Walker's	14	95	
36	Coneck, James †	"	Brookline	Prescott's	Gilbert's	15	745	
37	Cram, Asa ‡	"	Wilton	Reed's	Walker's	14	96	
38	Gray, Jonathan §	"	"	"	"	14	97	
39	McCrillis, William ‖	"	Nottingham	Stark's	Dearborn's	14	69	
40	Russell, Jason †	"	Nashua	Reed's	Walker's	14	95	
41	Wood, Oliver ‡	"	"	"	"	14	97	

* Died July 15. † Died July 24. ‡ State Papers, Vol. 14, p. 204, died before September 10. § State Papers, Vol. 13, p. 681, died before March 4, 1776. ‖ Died July 2.

No. 42. Broderick, Joseph, private, of Captain Daniel Moore's company, Stark's regiment, enlisted May 1, and disappeared from roll June 17, being allowed on roll, pay for one month and eighteen days, but it appears no one ever took his money. State Papers, Vol. 14, p. 70. Generally supposed to have been killed.

No. 43. Patten, James, private, of Captain John Marcy's company, Reed's regiment, enlisted May 10; allowed on roll, pay for one month and eleven days. On roll, died June 17.

No. 44. Melvin, John, private, of Captain John Marcy's company, Reed's regiment, enlisted May 25; allowed on roll, pay for twenty-four days. On roll, died June 17.

No. 45. Chamberlain, Benjamin, private, of Captain John Marcy's company, Reed's regiment, enlisted May 26; allowed on roll pay for one month and three days; died June 25. State Papers, Vol. 14, pp. 104, 105, for Nos. 43, 44, 45.

The last three men are supposed to have been wounded, and to have died, as on the same roll Joseph Farwell is marked killed June 17.

No. 46. Day, Stephen, private, Keene; Stark's regiment, Stiles's company; wounded, died August 17, 1775.

No. 47. McGrath, Daniel, private, Amherst; Prescott's regiment, Corey's company; wounded, died a prisoner, August 10, 1775. Name No. 9, page 90, Memorial Volume; the records regarding this man are a perfect puzzle.

No. 48. Minot, Joseph, corporal, Hollis; Prescott's regiment, Parker's company; killed. Name on the bronze tablets as from "*Westford*," Mass.; on original muster and pay roll, Hollis. He was taxed in Hollis in 1775. See History of Hollis, p. 138.

Bigelow, Benjamin, private, Nelson; Prescott's regiment, Wyman's company; wounded, prisoner in Boston jail and living September 14, 1775. Can any person give information what became of him?

No. 31. On original muster and pay roll—"David Scott, died June 2," or "22," in very pale ink; and of a recent date, apparently in a different handwriting and very dark ink, "Died June 16, 1775."

No. 32. "Joseph Taylor," on muster and pay roll, "enlisted June 13, and paid to Aug. 1." On October 6 reported "Dead"; date of death not given, and marked in pencil, "Killed."

All the foregoing forty-eight men's names, except Day's and Bigelow's, are on the Massachusetts memorial tablets.

Daniel Evans of Allenstown was a member of the Provincial Congress, sitting at Exeter in May, 1775. When that congress adjourned, he was known to have gone to Haverhill, Mass. A Daniel Evans of Captain Richardson's company was killed June 17, 1775, the name being No. 50 on the memorial tablets, residence unknown. As Daniel Evans never returned to Allenstown, he was presumably the man.

NEW HAMPSHIRE COLONIAL OR STATE RECORDS.

WHERE ARE THEY?

EXTER, March—7th 1783.

Sir When I had the honor to receive your favor of the 18th of December in which you nominate Stephen Gorham Esq. for Commissioner to Settle the accounts between this and the United States, etc. Our General Assembly was under an adjournment to the middle of February; as soon as they were convened I laid your Letter before them and they have approved of the Appointment as the inclosed Copy will Show.

I am Sir, with great Respect Your Obedient & Humbl Servt.

M. WEARE, *President.*

Honble Robert Morris, Esq: Copy.
—*State Papers, Vol. 10, p. 607.*

Thursday, June—19—1783.

Vote for the Committee of Safety to provide an office at Exeter for Mr. Gorham, the Commissioner appointed by Congress to settle accounts with this State.
—*State Papers, Vol. 8, p. 980.*

From the above, and it is all there is to be found, it is evident the government or congress of the United States assumed the indebtedness of New Hampshire, in part at least, for the expenses of the Revolutionary struggle for independence; and the question naturally arises, where are the records, muster and pay rolls? Were they not taken away by Gorham, and now in the possession of the government at Washington, or possibly destroyed by the British troops when they burned the government buildings at Washington in 1814?

Of Stark's regiment of thirteen companies, who participated in the battle of Bunker Hill, June 17, 1775, but two muster rolls, one original and one a copy, are known to be in existence,—the original, that of Captain Archelaus Townes, in the Historical Society rooms at Concord; the copy, that of Captain Gordon Hutchins's company, in Vol. 17, p. 3, State Papers—and not one original pay roll, only copies, and without the signatures of the men. Of Reed's regiment of ten companies, one muster roll— "Muster Roll of Captain Ezra Towne's Company in the Regiment of Foot, commanded by Colonel James Reed; belonging to the Army of the United Colonies of North America," a complete descriptive roll, giving the names of the men, rank, time of enlistment, where born, age, place of abode, occupation, height, color of the hair and eyes (See Vol. 16, p. 52, Mass. rolls)—is in existence; also the roll of Captain Hezekiah Hutchins's company (Vol. 14, p. 76) and copies of pay rolls without signatures of the men.

Perhaps the following record, never published before, may throw some light as to how Colonel Stark obtained his fifteen companies:

At a Meeting of the officers from the Province of N. Hampshire at Cambridge—April—26—1775.
Voted,—1. Col. John Hale—Chairman.
Voted,—2. Maj. Peter Coffin—Clerk.
Voted,—3. That the officers encourage their men to tarry here that incline until they hear from the Congress of N. Hampshire, and rely on the Honor of the Said province.
Voted,—4. That no officers take listing orders under the province of the Massachusetts Bay—till they hear from the Congress aforesaid.
Voted,—5. That the officers reccommend it to the Soldiers not to enlist under any officers belonging to the Bay Province, till they hear from Said Congress at N. Hampshire.
Voted,—6. That Col. John Stark take charge of the men till they hear from the Congress aforesaid.
A True Copy, Test.
PETER COFFIN, *Clerk*.

Col. John Stark had fifteen companies in his regiment up to June 12, when two companies, Whitcomb's and Thomas's, were transferred on that date to Col. James Reed—see Reed's letter to Committee of Safety, Province Papers, Vol. 7, page 518—and thirteen up to July 3 to 7. See Quartermaster Parkinson's accounts of rations issued to Colonel Stark's regiment, State Papers, Vol. 14, p. 153; also General Nathaniel Folsom,—"Chief Commander of the New Hampshire forces under the Commander-in-

Chief of the New England Army"—to Committee of Safety, dated Medford, June 23, 1775, where he was writing of Stark's regiment, "it still consisting of 13 companies," Province Papers, Vol. 7, p. 529; and the letter of General Henry Dearborn, who was a captain in Stark's regiment, afterwards secretary of war, and commander-in-chief of the American forces in the war of 1812, History of Nottingham, N. H., page 223.

General Washington took command of all the troops around Boston June 27, 1775; between that date and the 7th of July three more companies were transferred from Stark's regiment: One, Archelaus Townes's, 54 men, to Col. Ebenezer Bridge's Massachusetts regiment, and two, William Scott's, 64 men, and Jeremiah Stiles's, 72 men, to Col. Paul D. Sargent's Massachusetts regiment. Colonel Sargent was a resident of Amherst, N. H., but engaged in the service of Massachusetts.

Number of New Hampshire men on the Bunker Hill rolls, omitting all who were discharged prior to or enlisting after June 17, 1775: Stark's regiment, 842; Reed's regiment, 599; Massachusetts regiments, 210; total, 1,651; and in other Massachusetts regiments, not in the battle of Bunker Hill, same date, 317 New Hampshire men; total, 1,968; and June 22, Col. Enoch Poor arrived there with eight companies of his regiment.

There is great difficulty in locating the residence of the men, even when the town is given in the rolls, as there are 74 in Massachusetts and New Hampshire having the same name, and rising 100 changed from what they were in 1775.

Captain Bancroft's company from Dunstable, with 42 men from that town, in the battle of Bunker Hill—some were killed, others wounded. Dunstable was originally one town; in 1775, two, one in Massachusetts, the other in New Hampshire. The New Hampshire Dunstable is now Nashua.

New Hampshire paid two hundred and seventy pounds for ninety guns lost at the battle of Bunker Hill.

GEORGE C. GILMORE,
Special Commissioner,

MANCHESTER, February 12, 1891.

ELECTION SERMONS.

The annual election sermons for almost a half century of a state government under the constitution of 1784 were a conspicuous and respected feature of the inauguration ceremonies at the beginning of a political year. In their private and public relations, the clergy were held in high esteem, and the appointment of a preacher of the election sermon was a special recognition of eminence in the clerical profession. With the exception of 1793 a sermon was preached at each inauguration of a governor from 1784 to 1831, and in 1861, a critical period in the history of the state and nation, Rev. Henry E. Parker, D. D., preached the last election sermon in this historic series.

All the sermons, with the exception of the one preached in 1789 by Rev. Oliver Noble, and the one preached in 1795 by Rev. John Smith, were printed. Only a few complete sets of these sermons are preserved. A list of the preachers of election sermons follows:

1784	Samuel McClintock,	D. D.	Greenland,	Jer. xviii: 7-10
1785	Jeremy Belknap,	D. D.	Dover,	Ps. cxliv: 11-15
1786	Samuel Haven,	D. D.	Portsmouth,	Matt. xxiv: 45-47
1787	Jos. Buckminster,	D. D.	Portsmouth,	James i: 5
1788	Samuel Langdon,	D. D.	Hamp. Falls,	Deut. iv: 5-8
1789	Oliver Noble,		Newcastle.	
1790	John C. Ogden,	A. M.	Portsmouth,	Neh. v: 19
1791	Israel Evans,	A. M.	Concord,	Gal. v: 1
1792	William Morrison,	D. D.	Londonderry,	Rom. xiii: 3
1793	(No sermon preached).			
1794	Amos Wood,	A. B.	Weare,	Isaiah ix: 7
1795	John Smith,	A. M.	Hanover,	Isaiah xlvii: 8
1796	William F. Rowland,	A. M.	Exeter,	2 Sam. xxiii: 3
1797	Stephen Peabody,	A. M.	Atkinson,	Ex. xviii: 21

1798 Robert Gray,	A. M.	Dover,	Gen. xii: 2
1799 Seth Payson,	D. D.	Rindge,	Eccl. ix: 18
1800 Noah Worcester,	D. D.	Thornton,	Judges iii: 11
1801 Jacob Burnap,	D. D.	Merrimack,	Ps. lxxxvii: 4-6
1802 Joseph Woodman,	A. M.	Sanbornton,	Hosea vii: 9
1803 Aaron Hall,	A. M.	Keene,	2 Chron. xix: 6
1804 Nathaniel Porter,	D. D.	Conway,	1 Chron. xii: 32
1805 Reed Paige,	A. M.	Hancock,	Rom. xiii: 4
1806 James Miltimore,	A. M.	Stratham,	Job xxix: 14
1807 Nathan Bradstreet,	A. M.	Chester,	Luke vii: 4-5
1808 Asa McFarland,	D. D.	Concord,	2 Peter 1: 19
1809 William F. Rowland,	A. M.	Exeter,	Gal. v: 14
1810 Roswell Shurtleff,	A. M.	Hanover,	Rom. xiii: 1-5
1811 Thomas Beede,	A. M.	Wilton,	John vii: 1-5
1812 Moses Bradford,	A. M.	Francestown,	1 Tim. i: 15
1813 John H. Church,	D. D.	Pelham,	2 Chron. xv: 2
1814 Peter Holt,	A. M.	Epping,	Dan. ii: 44
1815 David Sutherland,		Bath,	Rev. i: 7
1816 Pliny Dickinson,		Walpole,	2 Chron. xxiv: 2
1817 Daniel Merrill,	A. M.	W. Nottingham,	Matt. vi: 10
1818 William Allen,	A. M.	Hanover,	Joshua i: 8
1819 Nathan Parker,	D. D.	Portsmouth,	John viii: 12
1820 James B. Howe,	A. M.	Claremont,	John ix: 29
1821 Ephr'm P. Bradford,	A. B.	New Boston,	Isaiah xxi: 11
1822 Jonathan French,	A. M.	No. Hampton,	2 Chron. i: 10
1823 Daniel Dana,	D. D.	Londonderry,	Prov. xiv: 34
1824 Bennet Tyler,	D. D.	Hanover,	Gen. xx: 11
1825 Phineas Cooke,	A. M.	Acworth,	Matt. xxii: 21
1826 Ferdinand Ellis,	A. M.	Exeter,	Ps. lxxxii: 6-7
1827 Nath'l W. Williams,	A. M.	Concord,	Matt. vi: 10
1828 Nathaniel Bouton,	A. M.	Concord,	Luke xix: 13
1829 Humphrey Moore,	A. M.	Milford,	1 Cor. xii: 21
1830 Jaazaniah Crosby,	A. M.	Charlestown,	Deut. xxviii: 1
1831 Nathan Lord,	D. D.	Hanover,	1 Cor. xiii: 5
1861 Henry E. Parker,	A. M.	Concord,	Jer. xviii: 7-10

No sermons were delivered between 1831 and 1861, and none after 1861.

www.ingramcontent.com/pod-product-compliance
Lightning Source LLC
Chambersburg PA
CBHW020859160426
43192CB00007B/996